Peopleware
Third Edition

Peopleware
Productive Projects and Teams
Third Edition

Tom DeMarco
Timothy Lister

✦Addison-Wesley

Upper Saddle River, NJ • Boston • Indianapolis • San Francisco
New York • Toronto • Montreal • London • Munich • Paris • Madrid
Capetown • Sydney • Tokyo • Singapore • Mexico City

CREDITS

For the cover art:
"One Sunday Afternoon I Took a Walk Through the Rose Garden, 1981" by Herbert Fink. Used by permission of Sarah Fink.

For the Dedication:
Excerpt from "The Wizard of Oz" granted courtesy of Warner Bros. Entertainment Inc., All Rights Reserved, © 1939.

For the excerpts in Chapter 3, from "Vienna" by Billy Joel:
Vienna
Copyright © 1979 IMPULSIVE MUSIC
All Rights Administered by ALMO MUSIC CORP.
All Rights Reserved. Used by Permission.
Reprinted by Permission of Hal Leonard Corporation.

For the excerpts and graphics in Chapter 13, Used by permission of Oxford University Press:
From The Oregon Experiment by Christopher Alexander et al. Copyright © 1975 by Christopher Alexander. From A Pattern Language by Christopher Alexander et al. Copyright © 1977 by Christopher Alexander. From The Timeless Way of Building by Christopher Alexander. Copyright © 1979 by Christopher Alexander.

For the excerpt in Chapter 15, from "Death of a Salesman" by Arthur Miller:
From DEATH OF A SALESMAN by Arthur Miller, copyright 1949, renewed © 1977 by Arthur Miller. Used by permission of Viking Penguin, a division of Penguin Group (USA) Inc. For distribution within the United Kingdom: Two lines from DEATH OF A SALESMAN by Arthur Miller. Copyright © 1949 by Arthur Miller, copyright renewed © 1977 by Arthur Miller, used by permission of The Wylie Agency LLC.

The publisher offers excellent discounts on this book when ordered in quantity for bulk purchases or special sales, which may include electronic versions and/or custom covers and content particular to your business, training goals, marketing focus, and branding interests. For more information, please contact:

U.S. Corporate and Government Sales
(800) 382-3419
corpsales@pearsontechgroup.com

For sales outside the United States, please contact:

International Sales
international@pearsoned.com

Visit us on the Web: informit.com/aw

Library of Congress Cataloging-in-Publication Data

DeMarco, Tom.
  Peopleware : productive projects and teams / Tom DeMarco, Timothy Lister. — Third edition.
       pages cm
Includes index.
ISBN13: 978-0-321-93411-6 (alk. paper)
ISBN10: 0-321-93411-3 (alk. paper)
1. Management. 2. Organizational behavior. 3. Organizational effectiveness. 4. Project management. I. Lister, Timothy R. II. Title.
HD31.D42218 2014
658.4'022--dc23   2013010087

ISBN-13: 978-0-321-93411-6
ISBN-10:   0-321-93411-3
Text printed in the United States on recycled paper at LSC Communications in Crawfordsville, Indiana.
15 2019

The Great Oz has spoken.
Pay no attention to that man behind the curtain.
The Great Oz has spoken.
—The Wizard of Oz

To all our friends and colleagues who have shown us
how to pay no attention to the man behind the curtain.

Contents

Preface

What we have come to think of as the Peopleware project began for us during the course of a long night flight over the Pacific more than thirty years ago. We were flying together from L.A. to Sydney to teach our Software Engineering Lectures series. Unable to sleep, we gabbed through the night about the deep complexities we were encountering in systems projects of our own and the ones related to us by our clients. One of us—neither one can remember which it was—reflected back over what we'd been discussing and offered this summing up: "Maybe . . . the major problems of systems work are not so much technological as sociological."

It took a while for that to sink in because it was so contrary to what had been our thinking before. We, along with nearly everyone else involved in the high-tech endeavors, were convinced that technology was all, that whatever your problems were, there had to be a better technology solution to them. But if what you were up against was inherently *sociological*, better technology seemed unlikely to be much help. If a group of people who had to work together didn't trust each other, for example, no nifty software package or gizmo was going to make a difference.

Once the idea was out in the open, we began to think up examples, and it soon became clear to both of us that the social complexities on most of the projects we'd known simply dwarfed any real technological challenges that the projects had had to deal with. And then, inevitably, we needed to face up to something far more upsetting: While we had probably known in our bones for a long time that sociology mattered more than technology, *neither of us had ever managed that way.* Yes, we had done things from time to time that helped teams work better together or that relaxed group tensions, but those things had never seemed like the essence of our work.

How would we have managed differently if we'd realized earlier that the human side mattered much more than the tech side? We started making lists. We had blank acetates and foil pens handy, and so we put some of the lists onto overhead slides and thought giddily of actually presenting some of these ideas to our Sydney audience. What the hell! Sydney was half a globe away from the States and Europe; if we bombed in Australia, who would ever know of it back home?

Our Sydney audience the next week was immediately engaged by the peopleware material, and a bit chagrined (evidently we weren't the only ones who had been managing as if only the technology really mattered). Best of all, people chimed in with lots of examples of their own, which we cheerfully appropriated.

What separated that early out-of-town tryout from the first edition of the book in 1987 was a ton of work conducting surveys and performing empirical studies to confirm what had been only suspicions about the effects of the environment (Part II of this third edition) and to validate some of our more radical suggestions about team dynamics and communication (most of the rest of the book).

Peopleware in its first two editions made us a kind of clearinghouse for ideas about the human side of technology projects, and so our thinking has had to expand to keep up. New sections in this third edition treat some pathologies of leadership that hadn't been judged pathological before, an evolving culture of meetings, hybrid teams made up of people from seemingly incompatible generations, and a growing awareness that, even now, some of our most common tools are more like anchors than propellers.

For this third edition, we are indebted to Wendy Eakin of Dorset House and Peter Gordon of Addison-Wesley for editing and shaping our manuscript. Thanks, too, to our long-time colleagues at The Atlantic Systems Guild—Peter Hruschka, Steve McMenamin, and James and Suzanne Robertson—for thirty years of ideas, brainstorms, debates, meals, and friendship.

—Tom DeMarco
Camden, Maine

—Tim Lister
New York, New York

February 2013

About the Authors

Tom DeMarco and Timothy Lister are principals of The Atlantic Systems Guild (www.systemsguild.com), a consulting firm specializing in the complex processes of system building, with particular emphasis on the human dimension. Together, they have lectured, written, and consulted internationally since 1979 on management, estimating, productivity, and corporate culture.

Tom DeMarco is the author or co-author of nine books on subjects ranging from development methods to organizational function and dysfunction, as well as two novels and a book of short stories. His consulting practice focuses primarily on expert witness work, balanced against the occasional project and team consulting assignment. Currently enjoying his third year teaching Ethics at the University of Maine, he lives in nearby Camden.

Photo of Tom DeMarco
by Hans-Rudolf Schulz

Timothy Lister divides his time between consulting, teaching, and writing. Based in Manhattan, Tim is co-author with Tom of *Waltzing With Bears: Managing Risk on Software Projects,* and of *Adrenaline Junkies & Template Zombies: Understanding Patterns of Project Behavior,* written with four other principals of The Atlantic Systems Guild. He is a member of the IEEE, the ACM, and the Cutter IT Trends Council, and is a Cutter Fellow.

Photo of Timothy Lister
by James Robertson

PART I

Managing the Human Resource

Most of us as managers are prone to one particular failing: a tendency to manage people as though they were modular components. It's obvious enough where this tendency comes from. Consider the preparation we had for the task of management: We were judged to be good management material because we performed well as doers, as technicians and developers. That often involved organizing our resources into modular pieces, such as software routines, circuits, or other units of work. The modules we constructed were made to exhibit a black-box characteristic, so that their internal idiosyncrasies could be safely ignored. They were designed to be used with a standard interface.

After years of reliance on these modular methods, small wonder that as newly promoted managers, we try to manage our human resources the same way. Unfortunately, it doesn't work very well.

In Part I, we begin to investigate a very different way of thinking about and managing people. That way involves specific accommodation to the very *nonmodular* character of the human resource.

1

Somewhere Today,
a Project Is Failing

Since the days when computers first came into common use, there must have been tens of thousands of accounts receivable programs written. There are probably a dozen or more accounts receivable projects underway as you read these words. And somewhere today, one of them is failing.

Imagine that! A project requiring no real technical innovation is going down the tubes. Accounts receivable is a wheel that's been reinvented so often that many veteran developers could stumble through such projects with their eyes closed. Yet these efforts sometimes still manage to fail. Suppose that at the end of one of these debacles, you were called upon to perform an autopsy. (It would never happen, of course; there is an inviolable industry standard that prohibits examining our failures.)

Suppose, before all the participants had scurried off for cover, you got a chance to figure out what had gone wrong. One thing you would *not* find is that the technology had sunk the project. Safe to say, the state of the art has advanced sufficiently so that accounts receivable systems are technically possible. Something else must be the explanation.

During the first decade of our Peopleware project, we conducted annual surveys of development projects and their results. We've measured project size, cost, defects, acceleration factors, and success or failure in meeting schedules. Eventually, we accumulated more than five hundred project histories, all of them from real-world development efforts.

We observe that about 15 percent of all projects studied came to naught: They were canceled or aborted or "postponed" or they delivered products that were never used. For bigger projects, the odds are even worse. Fully 25 percent of projects that lasted 25 work-years or more failed to complete. In the early surveys, we discarded these failed data points and analyzed the others. Since

3

1979, though, we've been contacting whoever is left of the project staff to find out what went wrong. For the overwhelming majority of the bankrupt projects we studied, *there was not a single technological issue to explain the failure.*

The Name of the Game

The cause of failure most frequently cited by our survey participants was "politics." But now observe that people tend to use this word rather sloppily. Included under "politics" are such unrelated or loosely related things as communication problems, staffing problems, disenchantment with the boss or with the client, lack of motivation, and high turnover. People often use the word *politics* to describe any aspect of the work that is people-related, but the English language provides a much more precise term for these effects: They constitute the project's *sociology.* The truly political problems are a tiny and pathological subset.

If you think of a problem as political in nature, you tend to be fatalistic about it. You know you can stand up to technical challenges, but honestly, who among us can feel confident in the realm of politics? By noting the true nature of a problem as sociological rather than political, you make it more tractable. Project and team sociology may be a bit outside your field of expertise, but not beyond your capabilities.

Whatever you name these people-related problems, they're more likely to cause you trouble on your next assignment than all the design, implementation, and methodology issues you'll have to deal with. In fact, that idea is the underlying thesis of this whole book:

> *The major problems of our work are not so much* technological *as* sociological *in nature.*

Most managers are willing to concede the idea that they've got more people worries than technical worries. *But they seldom manage that way.* They manage as though technology were their principal concern. They spend their time puzzling over the most convoluted and most interesting puzzles that their people will have to solve, almost as though they themselves were going to do the work rather than manage it. They are forever on the lookout for a technical whizbang that promises to automate away part of the work (see Chapter 6, "Laetrile," for more on this effect). The most strongly people-oriented aspects of their responsibility are often given the lowest priority.

Part of this phenomenon is due to the upbringing of the average manager. He or she was schooled in how the job is done, not how the job is managed.

It's a rare firm in which new managers have done anything that specifically indicates an ability or an aptitude for management. They've got little management experience and no meaningful practice. So how do new managers succeed in convincing themselves that they can safely spend most of their time thinking technology and little or no time thinking about the people side of the problem?

The High-Tech Illusion

Perhaps the answer is what we've come to think of as the High-Tech Illusion: the widely held conviction among people who deal with any aspect of new technology (as who of us does not?) that they are in an intrinsically high-tech business. They are indulging in the illusion whenever they find themselves explaining at a cocktail party, say, that they are "in computers," or "in telecommunications," or "in electronic funds transfer." The implication is that they are part of the high-tech world. Just between us, they usually aren't. The researchers who made fundamental breakthroughs in those areas are in a high-tech business. The rest of us are appliers of their work. We use computers and other new technology components to develop our products or to organize our affairs. Because we go about this work in teams and projects and other tightly knit working groups, we are mostly in the human communication business. Our successes stem from good human interactions by all participants in the effort, and our failures stem from poor human interactions.

The main reason we tend to focus on the technical rather than the human side of the work is not because it's more crucial, but because it's easier to do. Getting the new disk drive installed is positively trivial compared to figuring out why Horace is in a blue funk or why Susan is dissatisfied with the company after only a few months. Human interactions are complicated and never very crisp and clean in their effects, but they matter more than any other aspect of the work.

If you find yourself concentrating on the technology rather than the sociology, you're like the vaudeville character who loses his keys on a dark street and looks for them on the adjacent street because, as he explains, "The light is better there."

2

Make a Cheeseburger, Sell a Cheeseburger

Development is inherently different from production. But managers of development and allied efforts often allow their thinking to be shaped by a management philosophy derived entirely from a production environment.

Imagine for the moment that you're the manager of the local fast food franchise. It makes perfect sense for you to take any or all of the following efficient production measures:

- Squeeze out error. Make the machine (the human machine) run as smoothly as possible.

- Take a hard line about people goofing off on the job.

- Treat workers as interchangeable pieces of the machine.

- Optimize the steady state. (Don't even think about how the operation got up to speed, or what it would take to close it down.)

- Standardize procedure. Do everything by the book.

- Eliminate experimentation—that's what the folks at headquarters are paid for.

These would be reasonable approaches if you were in the fast food business (or any production environment), but you're not. The "make a cheeseburger, sell a cheeseburger" mentality can be fatal in your development area. It can only serve to damp your people's spirits and focus their attention away from the real problems at hand. This style of management will be directly at odds with the work.

To manage thinking workers effectively, you need to take measures nearly opposite those listed above. Our proposed opposite approaches are described in the following sections.

A Quota for Errors

For most thinking workers, making an occasional mistake is a natural and healthy part of their work. But there can be an almost Biblical association between error on the job and sin. This is an attitude we need to take specific pains to change.

Speaking to a group of software managers, we introduced a strategy for what we think of as *iterative design*. The idea is that some designs are intrinsically defect-prone; they ought to be rejected, not repaired. Such dead ends should be expected in the design activity. The lost effort of the dead end is a small price to pay for a clean, fresh start. To our surprise, many managers felt this would pose an impossible political problem for their own bosses: "How can we throw away a product that our company has paid to produce?" They seemed to believe that they'd be better off salvaging the defective version even though it might cost more in the long run.

Fostering an atmosphere that doesn't allow for error simply makes people defensive. They don't try things that may turn out badly. You encourage this defensiveness when you try to systematize the process, when you impose rigid methodologies so that staff members are not allowed to make any of the key strategic decisions lest they make them incorrectly. The average level of technology may be modestly improved by any steps you take to inhibit error. The team sociology, however, can suffer grievously.

The opposite approach would be to *encourage* people to make some errors. You do this by asking your folks on occasion what dead-end roads they've been down, and by making sure they understand that "none" is not the best answer. When people blow it, they should be congratulated—that's part of what they're being paid for.

Management: The Bozo Definition

Management is a complex enough thing to defy simple definition, but that nuance was lost on one senior manager we encountered at a professional society meeting in London. He summed up his entire view of the subject with this statement: "Management is kicking ass." This equates to the view that managers provide all the thinking and the people underneath them just carry out their bidding. Again, that might be workable for cheeseburger production, but not for any effort for which people do the work with their heads rather than their hands. Everyone in such an environment has got to have the brain in gear. You may be able to kick people to make them active, but not to make them creative, inventive, and thoughtful.

Even if kicking people in the backside did boost their short-term productivity, it might not be useful in the long run: There is nothing more discouraging to any worker than the sense that his own motivation is inadequate and has to be "supplemented" by that of the boss.

The saddest thing about this management approach is that it's almost always superfluous. You seldom need to take Draconian measures to keep your people working; most of them love their work. You may even have to take steps sometimes to make them work *less*, and thus get more meaningful work done (more about this idea in Chapter 3, "Vienna Waits for You").

The People Store

In a production environment, it's convenient to think of people as parts of the machine. When a part wears out, you get another. The replacement part is interchangeable with the original. You order a new one, more or less, by number.

Many development managers adopt the same attitude. They go to great lengths to convince themselves that no one is irreplaceable. Because they fear that a key person will leave, they force themselves to believe that there is no such thing as a key person. Isn't that the essence of management, after all, to make sure that the work goes on whether the individuals stay or not? They act as though there were a magical People Store they could call up and say, "Send me a new George Gardenhyer, but make him a little less uppity."

One of my clients brought a splendid employee into a salary review and was just amazed that the fellow wanted something other than money. He said that he often had good ideas at home but that his slow Internet connection was a real bother to use. Couldn't the company install a new line into his house and buy him a high-performance workstation? The company could. In subsequent years, it even built and furnished a small home office for the fellow. But my client is an unusual case. I wonder what a less-perceptive manager would have done. Too many managers are threatened by anything their workers do to assert their individuality.

—TRL

One example of just such a less-perceptive manager was a boss who showed extreme signs of being threatened by his people's individuality: He had one very talented worker on the road for much of the year visiting client sites and, as a result, living on an expense account. An analysis of the man's expense reports showed that his expenditures on food were way out of line with those of other travelers. He spent 50 percent more on food than the others did. In an indignant public memo, the boss branded the worker a "food criminal." Now, the worker's *total* expenditures weren't out of line; whatever extra he spent on food, he saved on something else. The man was not more expensive, he was just different.

The uniqueness of every worker is a continued annoyance to the manager who has blindly adopted a management style from the production world. The natural *people* manager, on the other hand, realizes that uniqueness is what makes project chemistry vital and effective. It's something to be cultivated.

A Project in Steady State Is Dead

Steady-state production thinking is particularly ill-suited to project work. We tend to forget that a project's entire purpose in life is to put itself out of business. The only steady state in the life of a project is rigor mortis. Unless you're riding herd on a canceled or about-to-be-canceled project, the entire focus of project management ought to be the *dynamics* of the development effort. Yet the way we assess people's value to a new project is often based on their steady-state characteristics: how much code they can write or how much documentation they can produce. We pay far too little attention to how well each of them *fits* into the effort as a whole.

I was teaching an in-house design course some years ago, when one of the upper managers buttonholed me to request that I assess some of the people in the course (his project staff). He was particularly curious about one woman. It was obvious he had his doubts about her: "I don't quite see what she adds to a project; she's not a great developer or tester or much of anything." With a little investigation, I turned up this intriguing fact: During her 12 years at the company, the woman in question had never worked on a project that had been anything other than a huge success. It wasn't obvious what she was adding, but projects always succeeded when she was around. After watching her in class for a week and talking to some of her co-workers, I came to the conclusion that she was a superb catalyst. Teams naturally jelled better when she was there. She helped people communicate with each other and get along. Projects were more fun when she was part of them. When I tried to explain this idea to the manager, I struck out. He just didn't recognize the role of catalyst as essential to a project.

—TDM

The catalyst is important because the project is always in a state of flux. Someone who can help a project to jell is worth two people who just do work.

We Haven't Got Time to Think about This Job, Only to Do It

If you are charged with getting a task done, what proportion of your time ought to be dedicated to actually doing the task? Not 100 percent. There ought to be some provision for brainstorming, investigating new methods, figuring out how to avoid doing some of the subtasks, reading, training, and just goofing off.

Looking back over our own years as managers, we've both concluded that we were off-track on this subject. We spent far too much of our time trying to get things done and not nearly enough time asking the key question, "Ought this thing to be done at all?" The steady-state cheeseburger mentality barely even pays lip service to the idea of thinking on the job. Its every inclination is to push the effort into 100-percent do-mode. If an excuse is needed for the lack of think-time, the excuse is always time pressure—as though there were ever work to be done without time pressure.

The importance of a more considered approach goes up sharply as the stakes increase. It's when the truly Herculean effort is called for that we have to learn to do work less of the time and think about the work more. The more heroic the effort required, the more important it is that the team members learn to interact well and enjoy it. The project that has to be done by an impossible fixed date is the very one that can't afford *not* to have frequent brainstorms and even a project dinner or some such affair to help the individual participants knit into an effective whole.

But all that is motherhood. Everybody knows that and acts accordingly, right? Wrong. We are so single-mindedly oriented toward Doing Something, Anything that we spend a scant 5 percent of our time on the combined activities of planning, investigating new methods, training, reading books, estimating, budgeting, scheduling, and allocating personnel. (The 5-percent figure comes from an analysis of system development projects, but it seems to apply more broadly than that, perhaps to the entire category of salaried workers.)

The statistics about reading are particularly discouraging: The average software developer, for example, doesn't own a single book on the subject of his or her work, and hasn't ever read one. That fact is horrifying for anyone concerned about the quality of work in the field; for folks like us who write books, it is positively tragic.

3

Vienna Waits for You

Some years ago, I was swapping war stories with the manager of a large project in Southern California. He began to relate the effect that his project and its crazy hours had had on his staff. There were two divorces that he could trace directly to the overtime his people were putting in, and one of his worker's kids had gotten into some kind of trouble with drugs, probably because his father had been too busy for parenting during the past year. Finally, there had been the nervous breakdown of the test-team leader.

As he continued through these horrors, I began to realize that in his own strange way, the man was bragging. You might suspect that with another divorce or two and a suicide, the project would have been a complete success, at least in his eyes.

—TDM

For all the talk about "working smarter," there is a widespread sense that what real-world management is all about is getting people to work harder and longer, largely at the expense of their personal lives. Managers are forever tooting their horns about the quantity of overtime their people put in, and the tricks one can use to get even more out of them.

Spanish Theory Management

Historians long ago formed an abstraction about different theories of value: The Spanish Theory, for one, held that only a fixed amount of value existed on earth, and therefore the path to the accumulation of wealth was to learn to extract it more efficiently from the soil or from people's backs. Then there

13

to extract it more efficiently from the soil or from people's backs. Then there was the English Theory that held that value could be created through ingenuity and technology. So the English had an Industrial Revolution, while the Spanish spun their wheels trying to exploit the land and the Indians in the New World. They moved huge quantities of gold across the ocean, and all they got for their effort was enormous inflation (too much gold money chasing too few usable goods).

The Spanish Theory of Value is alive and well among managers everywhere. You see that whenever they talk about productivity. Productivity ought to mean achieving more in an hour of work, but all too often it has come to mean extracting more for an hour of pay. There is a large difference. The Spanish Theory managers dream of attaining new productivity levels through the simple mechanism of unpaid overtime. They divide whatever work is done in a week by forty hours, not by the eighty or ninety hours that the worker actually put in.

That's not exactly productivity—it's more like fraud—but it's the state of the art for many American managers. They bully and cajole their people into long hours. They impress upon them how important the delivery date is (even though it may be totally arbitrary; the world isn't going to stop just because a project completes a month late). They trick them into accepting hopelessly tight schedules, shame them into sacrificing any and all to meet the deadline, and do anything to get them to work longer and harder.

And Now a Word from the Home Front

Although your staff may be exposed to the message "work longer and harder" while they're at the office, they're getting a very different message at home. The message at home is, "Life is passing you by. Your laundry is piling up in the closet, your babies are uncuddled, your spouse is starting to look elsewhere. There is only one time around on this merry-go-round called life, only one shot at the brass ring. And if you use your life up on C++ . . ."

> *But you know when the truth is told,*
> *That you can get what you want or you can just get old.*
> *You're going to kick off before you even get halfway through.*
> *When will you realize . . . Vienna waits for you?*
>
> —Billy Joel, "The Stranger"

The Vienna that waits for you, in Billy Joel's phrase, is the last stop on your personal itinerary. When you get there, it's all over. If you think your project members never worry about such weighty matters, think again.

Your people are very aware of the one short life that each person is allotted. And they know too well that there has got to be something more important than the silly job they're working on.

There Ain't No Such Thing as Overtime

Overtime for salaried workers is a figment of the naïve manager's imagination. Oh, there might be some benefit in a few extra hours worked on Saturday to meet a Monday deadline, but that's almost always followed by an equal period of compensatory "undertime" while the workers catch up with their lives. Throughout the effort, there will be more or less an hour of undertime for every hour of overtime. The trade-off might work to your advantage for the short term, but for the long term it will cancel out.

> *Slow down you crazy child,*
> *And take the phone off the hook and disappear for a while.*
> *It's all right. You can afford to lose a day or two.*
> *When will you realize . . . Vienna waits for you?*

Just as the unpaid overtime was largely invisible to the Spanish Theory manager (who always counts the week as forty hours regardless of how much time the people put in), so too is the undertime invisible. You never see it on anybody's time sheet. It's time spent on the phone or in bull sessions or just resting. Nobody can really work much more than forty hours, at least not continually and with the level of intensity required for creative intellectual work.

Overtime is like sprinting: It makes some sense for the last hundred yards of the marathon for those with any energy left, but if you start sprinting in the first mile, you're just wasting time. Trying to get people to sprint too much can only result in loss of respect for the manager. The best workers have been through it all before; they know enough to keep silent and roll their eyes while the manager raves on that the job has got to get done by April. Then they take their compensatory undertime when they can, and end up putting in forty hours of real work each week. The best workers react that way; the others are workaholics.

Workaholics

Workaholics will put in uncompensated overtime. They'll work extravagant hours, though perhaps with declining effectiveness. Put them under enough pressure and they will go a long way toward spoiling their personal lives. But only for a while. Sooner or later, the message comes through to even the most dedicated workaholic:

> *Slow down, you're doing fine,*
> *You can't be everything you want to be before your time.*
> *Although it's so romantic on the borderline tonight.*
> *But when will you realize . . . Vienna waits for you?*

Once that idea is digested, the worker is lost forever after to the project. The realization that one has sacrificed a more important value (family, love, home, youth) for a less important value (work) is devastating. It makes the person who has unwittingly sacrificed seek revenge. He doesn't go to the boss and explain calmly and thoughtfully that things have to change in the future—he just quits, another case of burnout. One way or the other, he's gone.

Workaholism is an illness, but not an illness like alcoholism that affects only the unlucky few. Workaholism is more like the common cold: Everyone has a bout of it now and then. Our purpose in writing about it here is not so much to discuss its causes and cures, but to address the simpler problem of how you, the manager, ought to deal with your workaholics. If you exploit them to the hilt in typical Spanish Theory fashion, you'll eventually lose them. No matter how desperately you need them to put in all those hours, you can't let them do so at the expense of their personal lives. The loss of a good person isn't worth it. This point goes beyond the narrow area of workaholism, into the much more complex subject of *meaningful* productivity.

Productivity: Winning Battles and Losing Wars

Next time you hear someone talking about productivity, listen carefully to hear if the speaker ever uses the term "employee turnover." Chances are that he or she will not. In years of hearing productivity discussed and in hundreds of articles about it, we have never encountered a single expert that had anything to say about the related subject of turnover. But what sense can it possibly make to discuss one without the other? Consider some of the things that organizations typically do to improve productivity:

- Pressure people to put in more hours.
- Mechanize the process of product development.
- Compromise the quality of the product (more about this in the next chapter).
- Standardize procedures.

Any of these measures can potentially make the work less enjoyable and less interesting. Hence, the process of improving productivity risks motivating employees to look for more satisfying work elsewhere. That doesn't say you can't improve productivity without paying a turnover price. It only says you need to take turnover into account whenever you set out to attain higher productivity. Otherwise, you may achieve an "improvement" that is more than offset by the loss of your key people.

Most organizations don't even keep statistics on turnover. Virtually none can tell you what replacement of an experienced worker costs. And whenever productivity is considered, it is done as though turnover were nonexistent or cost-free. The Eagle project at Data General was a case in point. The project was a Spanish Theory triumph: Workaholic project members put in endless unpaid overtime hours to push productivity to unheard of levels. At the end of the project, virtually the entire development staff quit. What was the cost of that? No one even figured it into the equation.

Productivity has to be defined as benefit divided by cost. The benefit is observed dollar savings and revenue from the work performed, and cost is the total cost, including replacement of any workers used up by the effort.

Reprise

One of my early consults was a project that was proceeding so smoothly that the project manager knew she would deliver the product on schedule. She was summoned in front of the management committee and was asked for a progress report. She said she could guarantee that her product would be ready by the deadline of March 1, exactly on time according to the original estimate. The upper managers chewed over that piece of unexpected good news and then called her in again the next day. Since she was on time for March 1, they explained, the deadline had been moved up to January 15.

—TRL

A schedule that the project could actually meet was of no value to those Spanish Theory managers, because it didn't put the people under pressure. Better to have a hopelessly impossible schedule to extract more labor from the workers.

Chances are, you've known one or more Spanish Theory managers during your career. It's all very well to smile at their short-sightedness, but don't let yourself off the hook too easily. Each of us has succumbed at one time or another to the short-term tactic of putting people under pressure to get them to work harder. In order to do this, we have to ignore their decreased effectiveness and the resultant turnover, but ignoring bad side effects is easy. What's not so easy is keeping in mind an inconvenient truth like this one:

> *People under time pressure don't work better—they just work faster.*

In order to work faster, they may have to sacrifice the quality of the product and of their own work experience.

4

Quality—If Time Permits

Twentieth-century psychological theory holds that man's character is dominated by a small number of basic instincts: survival, self-esteem, reproduction, territory, and so forth. These are built directly into the brain's firmware. You can consider these instincts intellectually without great passion (that's what you're doing now), but when you *feel* them, there is always passion involved. Even the slightest challenge to one of these built-in values can be upsetting.

Whenever strong emotions are aroused, it's an indication that one of the brain's instinctive values has been threatened. A novice manager may believe that work can be completed without people's emotions ever getting involved, but if you have any experience at all as a manager, you have learned the opposite. Our work gives us plenty of opportunity to exercise the emotions.

Chances are, you can think of at least one incident when a person's emotions did flare up as a direct result of something purely work-related. Consider that incident now and ask yourself (probably for the nth time), Where did all the emotion come from? Without knowing anything about your specific incident, we're willing to bet that threatened self-esteem was a factor. There may be many and varied causes of emotional reaction in one's personal life, but in the workplace, the major arouser of emotions is threatened self-esteem.

We all tend to tie our self-esteem strongly to the quality of the product we produce—not the *quantity* of product, but the *quality*. (For some reason, there is little satisfaction in turning out huge amounts of mediocre stuff, although that may be just what's required for a given situation.) Any step you take that may jeopardize the quality of the product is likely to set the emotions of your staff directly against you.

The Flight from Excellence

Managers jeopardize product quality by setting unreachable deadlines. They don't think about their action in such terms; they think rather that what they're doing is throwing down an interesting challenge to their workers, something to help them strive for excellence.

Experienced (jaded) workers know otherwise. They know that under the gun, their efforts will be overconstrained. There will be no freedom to trade off resources to make on-time delivery possible. They won't have the option of more people or reduced function. The only thing to give on will be quality. Workers kept under extreme time pressure will begin to sacrifice quality. They will push problems under the rug to be dealt with later or foisted off onto the product's end user. They will deliver products that are unstable and not really complete. They will hate what they're doing, but what other choice do they have?

The hard-nosed, real-world manager part of you has an answer to all this: "Some of my folks would tinker forever with a task, all in the name of 'Quality.' But the market doesn't give a damn about that much quality—it's screaming for the product to be delivered yesterday and will accept it even in a quick-and-dirty state." In many cases, you may be right about the market, but the decision to pressure people into delivering a product that doesn't measure up to their own quality standards is almost always a mistake.

We managers tend to think of quality as just another attribute of the product, something that may be supplied in varying degrees according to the needs of the marketplace. It's like the chocolate sauce you pour onto a homemade sundae: more for people who want more, and less for people who want less.

The builders' view of quality, on the other hand, is very different. Since their self-esteem is strongly tied to the quality of the product, they tend to impose quality standards of their own. The minimum that will satisfy them is more or less the best quality they have achieved in the past. This is invariably a higher standard than what the market requires and is willing to pay for.

"But the market doesn't give a damn about that much quality." Read those words and weep, because they are almost always true. People may talk in glowing terms about quality or complain bitterly about its absence, but when it comes time to pay the price for quality, their true values become apparent. On a software project, for instance, you might be able to make the following kind of presentation to your users: "We can extrapolate from empirical evidence that the Mean Time Between Failures for this product is now approximately 1.2 hours. So, if we deliver it to you today, on time, it will have very poor stability. If we put in another three weeks, we can forecast MTBF of approximately two thousand hours, a rather respectable result." Expect to see some Olympic-class hemming and hawing. The users will explain that they are as quality-conscious as the next fellow, but three weeks is real money.

Speaking of software, that industry has accustomed its clients to accept in-house-developed application programs with an average defect density of one to three defects per hundred lines of code! With sublime irony, this disastrous record is often blamed on poor quality consciousness of the builders. That is, those same folks who are chided for being inclined to "tinker forever with a program, all in the name of 'Quality'" are also getting blamed when quality is low. Let's put the blame where it belongs. He who pays the piper is calling for a low-quality tune. By regularly putting the development process under extreme time pressure and then accepting poor-quality products, the software user community has shown its true quality standard.

All of this may sound like a diatribe against software users and against the standards of the marketplace in general, but it needn't be taken that way. We have to assume that the people who pay for our work are of sound enough mind to make a sensible trade-off between quality and cost. The point here is that the client's perceived needs for quality in the product are often not as great as those of the builder. There is a natural conflict. Reducing the quality of a product is likely to cause some people not to buy, but the reduced market penetration that results from virtually any such quality reduction will often be more than offset by increased profit on each item sold.

Allowing the standard of quality to be set by the buyer, rather than the builder, is what we call *the flight from excellence*. A market-derived quality standard seems to make good sense only as long as you ignore the effect on the builder's attitude and effectiveness.

In the long run, market-based quality costs more. The lesson here is,

> *Quality, far beyond that required by the end user, is a means to higher productivity.*

If you doubt that notion, imagine the following gedankenexperiment: Ask a hundred people on the street what organization or culture or nation is famous for high quality. We predict that more than half the people today would answer, "Japan." Now ask a different hundred people what organization or culture or nation is famous for high productivity. Again, the majority can be expected to mention, "Japan." The nation that is an acknowledged quality leader is also known for its high productivity.

Wait a minute. How is it possible that higher quality coexists with higher productivity? That flies in the face of the common wisdom that adding quality to a product means you pay more to build it. For a clue, read the words of Tajima and Matsubara, two of the most respected commentators on the Japanese phenomenon:

> *The trade-off between price and quality does not exist in Japan. Rather, the idea that high quality brings on cost reduction is widely accepted.*[1]

Quality Is Free, But . . .

Philip Crosby presented this same concept in his book *Quality Is Free*, published in 1979. In this work, Crosby gave numerous examples and a sound rationale for the idea that letting the builder set a satisfying quality standard of his own will result in a productivity gain sufficient to offset the cost of improved quality.

We have an awful inkling that Crosby's book has done more harm than good in industry. The problem is that the great majority of managers haven't read it, but everybody has heard the title. The title has become the whole message. Managers everywhere are enthusing over quality: "The sky's the limit for quality, we'll have as much free quality as we can get!" This hardly boils down to a positive quality consciousness. The attitude is just the opposite of what Crosby advocates.

The real message of the linked quality and productivity effects needs to be presented in slightly different terms:

> *Quality is free, but only to those who are willing to pay heavily for it.*

The organization that is willing to budget only zero dollars and zero cents for quality will always get its money's worth. A policy of "Quality–If Time Permits" will assure that no quality at all sneaks into the product.

Hewlett-Packard has long been an example of an organization that reaps the benefits from increased productivity due to high, builder-set quality standards. From its beginning, the company has made a cult of quality. In such an environment, the argument that more time or money is needed to produce a high-quality product is generally not heard. The result is that developers know they are part of a culture that delivers quality beyond what the

---

1. D. Tajima and T. Matsubara, "Inside the Japanese Software Industry," *Computer*, Vol. 17 (March 1984), p. 40.

marketplace requires. Their sense of quality identification works for increased job satisfaction and some of the lowest turnover figures seen anywhere in the industry.

Power of Veto

In some Japanese companies, notably Hitachi Software and parts of Fujitsu, the project team has an effective power of veto over delivery of what they believe to be a not-yet-ready product. No matter that the client would be willing to accept even a substandard product, the team can insist that delivery wait until its own standards are achieved. Of course, project managers are under the same pressure there that they are here: They're being pressed to deliver something, anything, right away. But enough of a quality culture has been built up so that these Japanese managers know better than to bully their workers into settling for lower quality.

Could you give your people power of veto over delivery? Of course, it would take nerves of steel, at least the first time. Your principal concern would be that Parkinson's Law would be working against you. That's an important enough subject to warrant a chapter of its own.

5

Parkinson's Law Revisited

W riting in 1954, the British author C. Northcote Parkinson introduced the notion that work expands to fill the time allocated for it,
now known as Parkinson's Law.

If you didn't know that few managers receive any management training
at all, you might think there was a school they all went to for an intensive
course on Parkinson's Law and its ramifications. Even managers that know
they know nothing about management nonetheless cling to that one axiomatic truth governing people and their attitude toward work: Parkinson's Law.
It gives them the strongest possible conviction that the only way to get work
done at all is to set an impossibly optimistic delivery date.

Parkinson's Law and Newton's Law

Parkinson's Law is a long way from being axiomatic. It's not a law in the
same sense that Newton's law is a law. Newton was a scientist. He investigated the gravitational effect according to the strictest scientific method. His
law was only propounded after rigorous verification and testing. It has stood
the test of several centuries of subsequent study.

Parkinson was not a scientist. He collected no data; he probably didn't
even understand the rules of statistical inference. Parkinson was a humor-
ist. His "law" didn't catch on because it was so true. It caught on because it
was funny.

Of course, Parkinson's Law wouldn't be funny if there weren't a germ of
truth in it. Parkinson cites examples of his law as observed in a fictitious
government bureaucracy, some believe patterned on the British Post Office.

Bureaucracies are prone to such problems, because they give little job-derived satisfaction to their workers. But you probably don't work in a bureaucracy. Even if you do, you go to great lengths to make sure that your people are spared its effects; otherwise, they'd never get anything done. The result is that your people have the possibility of lots of job-derived satisfaction. That leads to a simple truth worth stating:

> *Parkinson's Law almost certainly doesn't apply to your people.*

Their lives are just too short to allow too much loafing on the job. Since they enjoy their work, they are disinclined to let it drag on forever—that would just delay the satisfaction they all hanker for. They are as eager as you are to get the job done, provided only that they don't have to compromise their standard of quality.

You Wouldn't Be Saying This If You'd Ever Met Our Herb

Every manager, at least some time in his or her life, has to deal with a worker who does seem to be avoiding work, or who seems to have no standard of quality, or who just can't get the job done. Doesn't that confirm Parkinson's Law?

In a healthy work environment, the reasons that some people don't perform are lack of competence, lack of confidence, and lack of affiliation with others on the project and the project goals. In none of these cases is schedule pressure liable to help very much. When a worker seems unable to perform and seems not to care at all about the quality of his work, for example, it is a sure sign that the poor fellow is overwhelmed by the difficulty of the work. He doesn't need more pressure. What he needs is reassignment, possibly to another company.

Even on the rare occasion when leaning on someone is the only option, the manager is the last person to do the leaning. It works far better when the message comes from the team. We've seen cases of well-knit teams in which the manager would have had to get in line to yell at the one person who wasn't pulling along with everyone else.

We'll have more to say in later chapters about teams and building a sensible chemistry for team formation. The point here is not what does work, but what doesn't: Treating your people as Parkinsonian workers doesn't work. It can only demean and demotivate them.

Some Data from the University of New South Wales

Of course, the Parkinson's Law mentality is not going to go away just because we say it ought to. What would help to convert managers would be some carefully collected data proving that Parkinson's Law doesn't apply to most workers. (Forget for a moment that Parkinson supplied no data at all to prove that the law did apply, he just reiterated it for a few hundred pages.)

Two respected researchers at the University of New South Wales, Michael Lawrence and Ross Jeffery, ran annual surveys through the eighties and nineties. They measured live projects in industry according to a common data collection standard. Each year they focused on a different aspect of project work. The 1985 survey provided some data that reflects on the inapplicability of Parkinson's Law. It isn't exactly the "smoking gun" that completely invalidates the law, but it ought to be sufficient to raise some doubts.

Lawrence and Jeffery set out to determine the productivity effect of various estimating methods. They had in mind to prove (or disprove) the folkloric belief that developers (programmers, in this case) work harder if they're trying to meet their own estimates. For each of 103 projects studied, Lawrence and Jeffery calculated a weighted metric of productivity. They then grouped the sample into subgroups, depending on how the original estimates were made. A partial result is presented in Table 5–1.

So far, the results confirm the folklore: Programmers seem to be a bit more productive after they've done the estimate themselves, compared to cases in which the manager did it without even consulting them. When the two did the estimating together, the results tended to fall in between.

In 21 projects studied that same year, estimates were prepared by a third party, typically a systems analyst. The developers in these cases substantially outperformed the projects in which estimating was done by a programmer and/or a supervisor (see Table 5–2).

These last data points do not confirm the folkloric view at all. Why should the programmers work harder to meet the analyst's estimate than they would for even their own? It may be tempting to explain this away as a simple

TABLE 5–1   Productivity by Estimation Approach (Partial Result)

Effort Estimate Prepared by	Average Productivity	Number of Projects
Programmer alone	8.0	19
Supervisor alone	6.6	3
Programmer & supervisor	7.8	16

TABLE 5-2   Productivity by Estimation Approach (Partial Result)

Effort Estimate Prepared by	Average Productivity	Number of Projects
Programmer alone	8.0	19
Supervisor alone	6.6	23
Programmer & supervisor	7.8	16
Systems analyst	9.5	21

anomaly in the data. But if you believe as we do that bad estimates are always a demotivating factor, then this data doesn't need explaining away at all. The systems analyst tends to be a better estimator than either the programmer or the supervisor. He or she typically knows the work in as much detail, but is not hampered by the natural optimism of the person who's actually going to do the job or the political and budgetary biases of the boss. Moreover, systems analysts typically have more estimating experience; they are able to project the effort more accurately because they've done more of it in the past and have thus learned their lessons.

Bad estimates, hopelessly tight estimates, sap the builders' energy. Capers Jones, known for his metric studies of development projects, puts it this way: "When the schedule for a project is totally unreasonable and unrealistic, and no amount of overtime can allow it to be made, the project team becomes angry and frustrated . . . and morale drops to the bottom."[1] It doesn't matter too terribly much whether the "totally unreasonable and unrealistic" schedule comes from the boss or from the builders themselves. People just don't work very effectively when they're locked into a no-win situation.

The most surprising part of the 1985 Jeffery-Lawrence study appeared at the very end, when they investigated the productivity of 24 projects for which no estimates were prepared at all. These projects far outperformed all the others (see Table 5-3).

Projects on which the boss applied no schedule pressure whatsoever ("Just wake me up when you're done.") had the highest productivity of all. Of course, none of this proves that Parkinson's Law doesn't apply to development workers. But doesn't it make you wonder?

The decision to apply schedule pressure to a project needs to be made in much the same way you decide whether or not to punish your child: If punishment is rare and your timing is impeccable so the justification is easily apparent, then maybe it can help. If you do it all the time, it's just a sign that you've got problems of your own.

---

1. Capers Jones, *Programming Productivity* (New York: McGraw-Hill, 1986), p. 213.

TABLE 5–3   Productivity by Estimation Approach (Full Result)

Effort Estimate Prepared by	Average Productivity	Number of Projects
Programmer alone	8.0	19
Supervisor alone	6.6	23
Programmer & supervisor	7.8	16
Systems analyst	9.5	21
(No estimate)	12.0	24

Variation on a Theme by Parkinson

A slight variation on Parkinson's Law produces something that is frighteningly true in many organizations:

Organizational busy work tends to expand to fill the working day.

This effect can start when the company is founded, and become worse every year. If the Dutch East India Company (founded in 1651 and once the largest company in the world) were still around, its employees might well be spending forty hours a week filling in forms. Notice that in this case, it's the company that exhibits Parkinsonian behavior rather than its employees. We'll return to this theme in Part II.

6

Laetrile

aetrile is a colorless liquid pressed from the soft bitter insides of apricot pits. In Sweden, you can buy the stuff in the grocery store for about the price of almond extract, and you use it in baking much as you would any other extract. In Mexico, you can buy it for fifty dollars a drop to "cure" your fatal cancer. Of course, it doesn't cure anything. All the evidence demonstrates that it is a cruel fraud. But since no one else has anything at all to offer them, some terminal patients accept the claims of the laetrile peddlers, no matter how outrageous. People who are desperate enough don't look very hard at the evidence.

Similarly, lots of managers are "desperate enough," and their desperation makes them easy victims of a kind of technical laetrile that purports to improve productivity. There is seldom any evidence at all to support the claims of what they buy. They, too, dispense with evidence because their need is so great.

Lose Fat While Sleeping

One day, in a moment of high silliness, I started clipping ads for products that claimed to boost productivity by 100 percent or more. Within a very short time, I had quite a pile. The amazing thing was the diversity of the means advertised to yield big productivity gains. There were seminars, packaged programs, methodologies, books, scheduling boards, hardware monitors, computing languages, and newsletters. Going uptown on the subway that night, I spotted one final ad on the back of the *New York Post*. It read, "Lose Fat While Sleeping." It seemed to fit right in with the others.

—TRL

We're all under a lot of pressure to improve productivity. The problem is no longer susceptible to easy solutions, because all the easy solutions were thought of and applied long ago. Yet some organizations are doing a lot better than others. We're convinced that those who do better are not using any particularly advanced technology. Their better performance can be explained entirely by their more effective ways of handling people, modifying the workplace and corporate culture, and implementing some of the measures that we'll discuss in Parts II through VI.

The relative inefficacy of technology may be a bit discouraging, at least in the short run, because the kinds of modification to corporate culture we advocate are hard to apply and slow to take effect. What would be far preferable is the coupon you cut out of the back pages of a magazine to send in with a few thousand bucks, so that some marvelous productivity gimmick will come back to you in the mail. Of course, it may not do much for you, but then easy nonsolutions are often more attractive than hard solutions.

The Seven Sirens

The false hopes engendered by easy technological nonsolutions are like those Sirens that tempted poor Odysseus. Each one reaches out to you with her own beguiling message, an attractive fallacy that leads nowhere. As long as you believe them, you're going to be reluctant to do the hard work necessary to build a healthy corporate culture.

The particular Sirens that plague you are a function of what industry you work in. We've identified seven from the field that we know best, software development, and we present them below, along with our own responses.

The Seven False Hopes of Software Management

- There is some new trick you've missed that could send productivity soaring.
  Response: You are simply not dumb enough to have missed something so fundamental. You are continually investigating new approaches and trying out the ones that make the most sense. None of the measures you've taken or are likely to take can actually make productivity soar. What they do, though, is to keep everybody healthy: People like to keep their minds engaged, to learn, and to improve. The line that there is some magical innovation out there that you've missed is a pure fear tactic, employed by those with a vested interest in selling it.

- Other managers are getting gains of 100 percent or 200 percent or more!
  Response: Forget it. The typical magical tool that's touted to you is focused on the coding and testing part of the life cycle. But even if coding and testing went away entirely, you couldn't expect a gain of 100 percent. There is still all the analysis, negotiation, specification, training, acceptance testing, conversion, and cutover to be done.

- Technology is moving so swiftly that you're being passed by.
  Response: Yes, technology is moving swiftly, but (the High-Tech Illusion again) most of what you're doing is not truly high-tech work. While the machines have changed enormously, the business of software development has been rather static. We still spend most of our time working on requirements and specification, the low-tech part of our work. Productivity within the software industry has improved by 3 to 5 percent a year, only marginally better than the steel or automobile industry.

- Changing languages will give you huge gains.
  Response: Languages are important because they affect the way you think about a problem, but again, they can have impact only on the implementation part of the project. Because of their exaggerated claims, some of our newer languages qualify as laetrile. Sure, it may be better to implement a new feature in Java, for example, rather than PHP, but even before Java came along, there were better ways to do whatever you needed to do: niche tools that made certain classes of function pretty easy to implement. Unless you've been asleep at the switch for the past few decades, change of a language won't do much for you. It might give you a 5-percent gain (nothing to sneeze at), but not more.

- Because of the backlog, you need to double productivity immediately.
  Response: The much talked about software backlog is a myth. We all know that projects cost a lot more at the end than what we expected them to cost at the beginning. So the cost of a system that didn't get built this year (because we didn't have the capacity for it) is optimistically assumed to be half of what it would actually cost to build, or even less. The typical project that's stuck in the mythical backlog is there because it has barely enough benefit to justify building it, even with the most optimistic cost assumptions. If we knew its real cost, we'd see that project for what it is: an economic loser. It shouldn't be in the backlog, it should be in the reject pile.

- You automate everything else; isn't it about time you automated away your software development staff?
  Response: This is another variation of the High-Tech Illusion: the belief that software developers do easily automatable work. Their principal work is human communication to organize the users' expressions of needs into formal procedure. That work will be necessary no matter how we change the life cycle. And it's not likely to be automated.

- Your people will work better if you put them under a lot of pressure.
  Response: They won't—they'll just enjoy it less.

So far, all this is rather negative. If leaning on people is counterproductive, and installing the latest technological doodad won't help much either, then what is the manager supposed to do?

This Is Management

In my early years as a developer, I was privileged to work on a project managed by Sharon Weinberg, later to become president of the Codd and Date Consulting Group. She was a walking example of much of what I now think of as enlightened management. One snowy day, I dragged myself out of a sickbed to pull together our shaky system for a user demo. Sharon came in and found me propped up at the console. She disappeared and came back a few minutes later with a container of soup. After she'd poured it into me and buoyed up my spirits, I asked her how she found time for such things with all the management work she had to do. She gave me her patented grin and said, "Tom, this is management."

—TDM

Sharon knew what all good instinctive managers know: The manager's function is not to make people work, but to make it possible for people to work.

PART II

The Office Environment

In order to make it possible for people to work, you have to come to grips
with those factors that sometimes make it impossible. The causes of lost
hours and days are numerous but not so different from one another. They
are often—maybe even most often—failures, in one form or another, of the
environment that the organization has provided to help you work. The phone
rings off the hook, the printer service man stops by to chat, the copier breaks
down, the chap from the blood drive calls to revise donation times, Personnel
continues to scream for the updated skills survey forms, time sheets are due
at 3 P.M., lots more phone calls come in, . . . and the day is gone. Some days
you never spend a productive minute on anything having to do with getting
actual work done.

It wouldn't be so bad if all these diversions affected the manager alone,
while the rest of the staff worked on peacefully. But as you know, it doesn't
happen that way. Everybody's workday is plagued with frustration and interruption. Entire days are lost, and nobody can put a finger on just where they
went. If you wonder why almost everything is behind schedule, consider this:

> There are a million ways to lose a workday, but not even a single
> way to get one back.

In Part II, we'll look into some of the causes of lost time and propose measures that you can take to create a healthy, work-conducive environment.

7

The Furniture Police

Suppose that in addition to your present duties, you were made responsible for space and services for your people. You would have to decide on the kind of workplace for each person, and the amount of space and expense to be allocated. How would you go about it? You'd probably want to study the ways in which people use their space, the amount of table space required, and the number of hours in a day spent working alone, working with one other person, and so forth. You'd also investigate the impact of noise on people's effectiveness. After all, your folks are *intellect workers*—they need to have their brains in gear to do their work, and noise does affect their ability to concentrate.

For each of the observed kinds of disturbance, you'd look for any easy, mechanical way to protect your workers. Given a reasonably free hand, you would investigate the advantages of closed space (one- and two- and three-person offices) versus open space. This would allow you to make a sensible trade-off of cost against privacy and quiet. Finally, you would take into account people's social needs and provide some areas where a conversation could take place without disturbing others.

It should come as no surprise to you that the people who do control space and services for your company (particularly if it's a large company) don't spend much time thinking about any of the concerns listed above. They don't collect any raw data; they don't strive to understand complex issues like productivity. Part of the reason for this is that they are not themselves doing the kind of work likely to suffer from a poor environment. They often constitute a kind of Furniture Police, whose approach to the problem is nearly the opposite of what your own would be.

The Police Mentality

The head of the Furniture Police is that fellow who wanders through the new office space the day before your staff is supposed to move in, with thoughts like these running through his head: "Look at how beautifully uniform everything is! You have no way to tell whether you're on the fifth floor or the sixth! But once those people move in, it will all be ruined. They'll hang up pictures and individualize their little modules, and they'll be *messy*. They'll probably want to drink coffee over my lovely carpet and even eat their lunch right here (shudder). Oh dear, oh dear, oh dear . . ." This is the person who promulgates rules about leaving each desk clean at night and prohibiting anything to be hung on the partitions except perhaps a company calendar. The Furniture Police at one company we know even listed a number for spilled coffee on the Emergency Numbers decal affixed to every phone. We were never there when anyone called the number, but you could probably expect white-coated maintenance men to come careening through the halls in an electric cart with flashing lights and a siren going ooogah-ooogah.

While on break at a seminar, a fellow told me that his company doesn't allow anything to be left on the desk at night except for a five-by-seven photo of the worker's family. Anything else and in the morning you'll find stuck to your desktop a nasty note (on corporate letterhead yet) from the Furniture Police. One guy was so offended by these notes that he could barely restrain his anger. Knowing how he felt, his fellow workers played a joke on him: They bought a picture frame from the local five-and-dime store, choosing one with a photograph of an all-American family as a sample. Then they replaced the photo of his own family with the other. Under the photo was what looked like a note from the Furniture Police, stating that since his family didn't pass muster by the corporate standards, he was being issued an "official company family photo" to leave on his desk.

—TRL

The Uniform Plastic Basement

To get a better feeling for the police mentality, look at the floor plan of Figure 7–1, now becoming common in organizations all over America.

This scheme deals forthrightly with the complicated question of who should have windowed space: no one. The trouble with windows is that there aren't enough of them to give one to every worker. If some people have windows and others do not, you'll be able to tell that you're in George's work space, for instance, by simple observation. We can't have that, now, can we?

Figure 7–1   Typical office floor plan.

But look at the side effect. The most frequently traveled paths, from elevator to cubicle or from cubicle to cubicle, do not pass in front of any window. Where such floor plans are used, the windows are not utilized at all; the window corridors are always empty. We first encountered the window corridor plan on the twentieth floor of a new skyscraper—there were magnificent views in every direction, views that virtually nobody ever saw. The people in that building may as well have worked in a basement.

Basement space is really preferable from the point of view of the Furniture Police, because it lends itself more readily to uniform layouts. But people work better in natural light. They feel better in windowed space and that feeling translates directly into higher quality of work. People don't want to work in a perfectly uniform space either. They want to shape their space to their own convenience and taste. These inconvenient facts are typical of a general class of inconveniences that come from dealing with human workers.

Visiting a few dozen different organizations each year, as we do, quickly convinces you that ignoring such inconvenient facts is intrinsic to many office plans. Almost without exception, the work space given to intellect workers is noisy, interruptive, un-private, and sterile. Some are prettier than others, but not much more functional. No one can get much real work done there. The very person who could work like a beaver in a quiet little cubbyhole with two large folding tables and a door that shuts is given instead an EZ-Whammo Modular Cubicle with 73 plastic appurtenances. Nobody shows much interest in whether it helps or hurts effectiveness.

All this may seem a bit harsh on those solid citizens who plan America's office space. If you think so, consider one last manifestation of the mindset of these planners. It is something so monstrous that you have to wonder why it's tolerated at all: the company paging system. Hard as this may be to believe, some companies actually use a public address system to interrupt perhaps thousands of workers—people who are trying to *think*—in order to locate one: *BONG! [static] ATTENTION, ATTENTION! PAGING PAUL POR-TULACA. WILL PAUL PORTULACA PLEASE CALL THE PAGING CENTER.* If you position yourself well, you can sometimes see thirty or forty salaried workers raise their heads at the initial bong and listen politely through the whole message, then look down again wondering what they were doing before they were interrupted.

Police-mentality planners design workplaces the way they would design prisons: optimized for containment at minimal cost. We have unthinkingly yielded to them on the subject of workplace design, yet for most organizations with productivity problems, there is no more fruitful area for improvement than the workplace. As long as workers are crowded into noisy, sterile, disruptive space, it's not worth improving anything *but* the workplace.

8

"You Never Get Anything Done around Here between 9 and 5."

Part of the folklore among development workers in all sectors of our economy is, "Overtime is a fact of life." This implies that the work can never get done in the amount of time worth allocating for it. That seems to us a rather dubious proposition. Overtime is certainly a fact of life in the software industry, for example, but that industry could hardly have come through a period of such phenomenal prosperity if the software built on the whole weren't worth a lot more than was paid for it. How to explain then the fact that software people as well as workers in other thought-intensive positions are putting in so many extra hours?

A disturbing possibility is that overtime is not so much a means to increase the *quantity* of work time as to improve its average *quality*. You hear evidence that this is true in such frequently repeated statements as these:

> *"I get my best work done in the early morning, before anybody else arrives."*

> *"In one late evening, I can do two or three days' worth of work."*

> *"The office is a zoo all day, but by about 6 P.M., things have quieted down and you can really accomplish something."*

To be productive, people may come in early or stay late or even try to escape entirely, by staying home for a day to get a critical piece of work done. One of our seminar participants reported that her new boss wouldn't allow her to work at home, so on the day before an important report was due, she took a sick day to get it done.

Staying late or arriving early or staying home to work in peace is a damning indictment of the office environment. The amazing thing is not that it's so often impossible to work in the workplace; the amazing thing is that everyone knows it and nobody ever does anything about it.

A Policy of Default

A California company that I consult for is very much concerned about being responsive to its people. One year, the company's management conducted a survey in which all programmers (more than a thousand) were asked to list the best and the worst aspects of their jobs. The manager who ran the survey was very excited about the changes the company had undertaken. He told me that the number two problem was poor communication with upper management. Having learned that from the survey, the company set up quality circles, gripe sessions, and other communication programs. I listened politely as he described them in detail. When he was done, I asked what the number one problem was. "The environment," he replied. "People were upset about the noise." I asked what steps the company had taken to remedy that problem. "Oh, we couldn't do anything about that," he said. "That's outside our control."

—TDM

All the more discouraging is that the manager wasn't even particularly embarrassed about failing to take steps to improve the environment. It was as though the programmers had complained that there was too much gravity, and management had decided after due reflection that they couldn't really do much about it; it was a problem whose solution was beyond human capacity. This is a policy of total default.

Changing the environment is not beyond human capacity. Granted, there is a power group in almost every company, a Furniture Police group, that has domain over the physical environment. But it's not impossible to make them see reason or to wrest control away from them. For the rest of this chapter, we'll present some of the reasons why you're going to have to do exactly that. In subsequent chapters, we'll give some hints about how to go about it.

Coding War Games: Observed Productivity Factors

From the years just before the first edition of this book, we have conducted some sort of a public productivity survey each year. So far, more than three hundred organizations worldwide have participated in these studies. Eventually, we began to run our annual survey as a sort of public competition in which teams of software implementors from different organizations compete to complete a series of benchmark coding and testing tasks in minimal time and with minimal defects. We call these competitions Coding War Games. Here's how they work:

- The basic competing unit is a pair of implementors from the same organization. The pair members do not work together, but in fact members work against each other as well as against all the other pairs.

- Both pair members perform exactly the same work, designing, coding, and testing a medium-sized program to our fixed specification.

- As they go through the exercise, participants record the time spent on a time log.

- After all participant testing is completed, the products are subjected to our standard acceptance test.

- Participants work in their own work areas during normal work hours using the same languages, tools, terminals, and computers that they use for any other project.

- All results are kept confidential.

From 1984 to 1986, more than six hundred developers from 92 companies participated in the games. The benefit to the individual is learning how he or she compares with the rest of the competitors. The benefit to the company is learning how well it does against other companies in the sample. And the benefit to us is learning a lot about what factors affect productivity, factors discussed in the rest of this chapter.

Individual Differences

One of the first results of the coding wars was proof of a huge difference between competing individuals. Of course, this had been observed before. Figure 8–1, for example, is a composite of the findings from three different sources on the extent of variation among individuals.

Three rules of thumb seem to apply whenever you measure variations in performance over a sample of individuals.

- Count on the best people outperforming the worst by about 10:1.

- Count on the best performer being about 2.5 times better than the median performer.

- Count on the half that are better-than-median performers outdoing the other half by more than 2:1.

These rules apply for virtually any performance metric you define. So, for instance, the better half of a sample will do a given job in less than half the time the others take; the more defect-prone half will put in more than two thirds of the defects, and so on.

Results of the Coding War Games were very much in line with this profile. Take as an example Figure 8–2, which shows the performance spread of time to achieve the first milestone (clean compile, ready for test) in one year's games.

Figure 8–1   Productivity variation among individuals.

Figure 8-2   Individual variation in performance.

The best performance was 2.1 times better than the average. The half above the median outperformed the half below the median by 1.9 to 1. Results of the subsequent games have been nearly identical.

Productivity Nonfactors

In our analysis of game results, we discovered that the following factors had little or no correlation to performance:

- **Language:** Those who coded in old languages like COBOL and Fortran did essentially as well as those who coded in Pascal and C. The spread within each language group was much like the overall spread of performance. The only exception to this observation about language was assembly language: The assembly language participants got badly left behind by all the other language groups. (But, then, people who use assembly language are used to being left behind.)

- **Years of experience:** People who had ten years of experience did not outperform those with two years of experience. There was no correlation between experience and performance except that those with less than six months' experience with the language used in the exercise did not do as well as the rest of the sample.

- **Number of defects:** Nearly a third of the participants completed the exercise with zero defects. As a group, the zero-defect workers paid no performance penalty for doing more precise work. (In fact, they took slightly less time, on the average, to complete the exercise than those who had one or more defects.)

- **Salary:** Salary levels varied widely over the sample. There was a very weak relationship between salary and performance. The half above the median made less than 10 percent more than the half below, but they performed nearly twice as well. The performance spread at any given salary level was nearly as wide as over the whole sample.

Again, nothing very astonishing, as most of these effects have been noted before. Slightly more surprising were some of the factors that we found *did* have a substantial effect on performance.

You May Want to Hide This from Your Boss

Among our findings of what did correlate positively to good performance was this rather unexpected one: *It mattered a lot who your pair mate was.* If you were paired with someone who did well, you did well, too. If your pair mate took forever to finish, so did you. If your pair mate didn't finish the exercise at all, you probably didn't either. For the average competing pair, the performances differed by only 21 percent.

Now, why is that so important? Because even though the pairs didn't work together, the two members of the pair came from the same organization. (In most cases, they were the only ones from that organization.) They worked in the same physical environment and shared the same corporate culture. The fact that they had nearly identical performances suggests that the wide spread of capabilities observed across the whole sample may not apply within the organization: Two people from the same organization tend to perform alike. That means the best performers are clustering in some organizations while the worst performers are clustering in others. This is the effect that software pioneer Harlan Mills predicted in 1981:

> *While this [10 to 1] productivity differential among programmers is understandable, there is also a 10 to 1 difference in productivity among software organizations.*[1]

Our study found that there were huge differences between the 92 competing organizations. Over the whole sample, the best organization (the one with the best average performance of its representatives) worked more than ten times faster than the worst organization. In addition to their speed, all com-

---

1. H. D. Mills, *Software Productivity* (New York: Dorset House Publishing, 1988), p. 266.

petitors from the fastest organization developed code that passed the major acceptance test.

This is more than a little unsettling. Managers for years have affected a certain fatalism about individual differences. They reasoned that the differences were innate, so you couldn't do much about them. It's harder to be fatalistic about the clustering effect. Some companies are doing a lot worse than others. Something about their environment and corporate culture is failing to attract and keep good people or is making it impossible for even good people to work effectively.

Effects of the Workplace

The bald fact is that many companies provide developers with a workplace that is so crowded, noisy, and interruptive as to fill their days with frustration. That alone could explain reduced efficiency as well as a tendency for good people to migrate elsewhere.

The hypothesis that qualities of the workplace may have a strong correlation to developer effectiveness is an easy one to test. All you have to do is devise a set of fixed benchmark tasks, similar to those that developers do in their normal work, and observe how well they perform each of these tasks in different environments. The Coding War Games were designed with exactly that purpose in mind.

In order to gather some data on the workplace, we had each war game participant (prior to the exercise) fill out a questionnaire about the physical quarters in which the work was to be performed. We asked for some objective data (measurements of the dedicated space provided and the height of partitions, for example) and for answers to some subjective questions like "Does your workplace make you feel appreciated?" and "Is your workplace acceptably quiet?" Then we correlated their answers to their performance in the exercise.

An easy way to spot the trend is to look at the workplace characteristics of people who did well in the exercise (based on a composite performance parameter) against those of participants who didn't do so well. We chose to compare the top quarter of finishers with the bottom quarter. Average performance of those in the top quarter was 2.6 times better than that of those in the bottom quarter. The environmental correlations are summarized in Table 8–1.

The top quartile, those who did the exercise most rapidly and effectively, work in space that is substantially different from that of the bottom quartile. The top performers' space is quieter, more private, better protected from interruption, and there is more of it.

TABLE 8-1   Environments of the Best and Worst Performers in the Coding War Games

Environmental Factor	Those Who Performed in 1st Quartile	Those Who Performed in 4th Quartile
1. How much dedicated work space do you have?	78 sq. ft.	46 sq. ft.
2. Is it acceptably quiet?	57% yes	29% yes
3. Is it acceptably private?	62% yes	19% yes
4. Can you silence your phone?	52% yes	10% yes
5. Can you divert your calls?	76% yes	19% yes
6. Do people often interrupt you needlessly?	38% yes	76% yes

What Did We Prove?

The data presented above does not exactly prove that a better workplace will help people to perform better. It may only indicate that people who perform better tend to gravitate toward organizations that provide a better workplace. Does that really matter to you? In the long run, what difference does it make whether quiet, space, and privacy help your current people to do better work or help you to attract and keep better people?

If we proved anything at all, it's that a policy of default on workplace characteristics is a mistake. If you participate in or manage a team of people who need to use their brains during the workday, then the workplace environment is your business. It isn't enough to observe, "You never get anything done around here between 9 and 5," and then turn your attention to something else. It's dumb that people can't get work done during normal work hours. It's time to do something about it.

9

Saving Money on Space

If your organization is anything like those studied in our last three annual surveys, the environmental trend is toward less privacy, less dedicated space, and more noise. Of course, the obvious reason for this is cost. A penny saved on the work space is a penny earned on the bottom line, or so the logic goes. Those who make such a judgment are guilty of performing a cost/benefit study without benefit of studying the benefit. They know the cost but haven't any idea what the other side of the equation may be. Sure, the savings of a cost-reduced workplace are attractive, but compared to what? The obvious answer is that the savings have to be compared to the risk of lost effectiveness.

Given the current assault on workplace costs, it's surprising how little the potential savings are compared to the potential risk. The entire cost of work space for one developer is a small percentage of the salary paid to the developer. How small depends on such factors as real-estate values, salary levels, and lease versus buy tactics. In general, it varies in the range from 6 to 16 percent. For a programmer/analyst working in company-owned space, you should expect to pay fifteen dollars directly to the worker for every dollar you spend on space and amenities. If you add the cost for employee benefits, the total investment in the worker could easily be twenty times the cost of his or her workplace.

The 20:1 ratio implies that workplace cost reduction is risky. Attempts to save a small portion of the one dollar may cause you to sacrifice a large portion of the twenty. The prudent manager could not consider moving people into cheaper, noisier, and more crowded quarters without first assessing whether worker effectiveness would be impaired. So, you might expect that the planners who have undertaken a decade-long program to change our office space into the voguish open-plan format must first have done some very careful productivity analysis. Not to do so would have demonstrated an irresponsible unconcern for the environment.

A Plague upon the Land

Irresponsible unconcern for the environment is, unfortunately, the norm for our times. We show it in the despoliation of our natural resources, so why not in workplace design? In a prophetic science fiction story, John Brunner describes pollution of the air, soil, and water continuing through the end of the next century. No matter how bad the pollution gets, almost no one complains. Like a vast herd of imperturbable sheep, the inhabitants of Brunner's world try to ignore the problem until, finally, all possibility for survival is lost. Then and only then do they take notice. Brunner called his book *The Sheep Look Up.*

American office workers have barely looked up while their work quarters have been degraded from sensible to silly. Not so long ago, they worked in two- and three-person offices with walls, doors, and windows. (You remember walls, doors, and windows, don't you?) In such space, one could work in quiet or conduct meetings with colleagues without disrupting neighbors.

Then, without warning, open-plan seating was upon us like a plague upon the land. The advocates of the new format produced not one shred of evidence that effectiveness would not be impaired. They really couldn't. Meaningful measurement of productivity is a complex and elusive thing. It has to be performed differently in each different work sector. It takes expertise, careful study, and lots of data collection.

The people who brought us open-plan seating simply weren't up to the task. But they *talked* a good game. They sidestepped the issue of whether productivity might go down by asserting very loudly that the new office arrangement would cause productivity to *go up,* and up a lot, by as much as 300 percent. They published articles, many of them crafted from the purest sculpted smoke. They gave their pronouncements impressive titles like this one from *Data Management* magazine: "Open-Plan DP Environment Boosts Employee Productivity." After that promising title, the author got right to the heart of the matter:

> *The fundamental areas of consideration in designing an open-plan office within an information processing environment are: the system's electrical distribution capabilities, computer support capabilities and manufacturer and dealer service.*

Period. That's it. That's all of the "fundamental areas of consideration." No mention of the fact that a *person* is going to be trying to work in that space.

Also missing from that article and from others like it is any notion of what employee productivity is all about. There was no evidence in the *Data Management* article to support the title. The only method we have ever seen used to confirm claims that the open plan improves productivity is *proof by repeated assertion.*

We Interrupt This Diatribe to Bring You a Few Facts

Before drawing the plans for its Santa Teresa facility, IBM violated all industry standards by carefully studying the work habits of those who would occupy the space. The study was designed by the architect Gerald McCue with the assistance of IBM area managers.[1] Researchers observed the work processes in action in current work spaces and in mock-ups of proposed work spaces. They watched programmers, engineers, quality control workers, and managers go about their normal activities. From their studies, they concluded that a minimum accommodation for the mix of people slated to occupy the new space would be the following:

- 100 square feet of dedicated space per worker

- 30 square feet of work surface per person

- Noise protection in the form of enclosed offices or 6-foot-high partitions (they ended up with about half of all professional personnel in enclosed one- and two-person offices)

The rationale for building the new laboratory to respect these minimums was simple: People in the roles studied *needed* the space and quiet in order to perform optimally. Cost reduction to provide work space below the minimum would result in a loss of effectiveness that would more than offset the cost savings. Other studies have looked into the same questions and come up with more or less the same answers. The McCue study was different only in one respect: IBM actually followed the recommendations and built a workplace where people can work. (We predict this company will go far.)

---

1. G. McCue, "IBM's Santa Teresa Laboratory," *IBM Systems Journal,* Vol. 17, No. 1 (1978), pp. 320–41.

Figure 9–1   Range of dedicated floor space.

How does the rest of the world match up to IBM's minimum standard workplace? Figure 9–1 shows a distribution of dedicated space per person computed across participants in our Coding War Game surveys.

Only 16 percent of participants had 100 square feet or more of work space. Only 11 percent of participants worked in enclosed offices or with greater than 6-foot-high partitions. There were more participants in the 20- to 30-square-foot group than in the 100-square-foot group. (With less than 30 square feet, you're trying to work in a total floor space less than the table space provided at Santa Teresa.)

Across the whole Coding War Games sample, 58 percent complained that their workplace was not acceptably quiet; 61 percent complained that it wasn't sufficiently private; 54 percent reported that they had a workplace at home that was better than the workplace provided by the company.

Workplace Quality and Product Quality

Companies that provide a small and noisy workplace are comforted by the belief that these factors don't really matter. They explain away all the complaints about noise, for instance, as workers campaigning for the added status of bigger, more private space. After all, what difference could a little noise make? It's just something to help keep people awake.

In order to determine whether attitude toward noise level had any correlation to work, we divided our sample into two parts, those who found the workplace acceptably quiet and those who didn't. Then we looked at the number of workers within each group who had completed the entire exercise without a single defect.

> *Workers who reported before the exercise that their workplace was acceptably quiet were* one-third more likely *to deliver zero-defect work.*

As the noise level gets worse, this trend seems to get stronger. For example, one company that was represented by fifty participants had an unacceptable noise rating 22-percent higher than average. At that company, those who did zero-defect work came disproportionately from the subset that found the noise level acceptable:

> *Zero-defect workers: 66 percent reported noise level okay*
>
> *One-or-more-defect workers: 8 percent reported noise level okay*

Again, as with the other environmental correlations, we asked that participants assess the noise level in their environments before performing the exercise.

Note that we made no objective measurements of noise levels. We simply asked people whether they found the noise level acceptable or not. As a result, we cannot distinguish between those who worked in a genuinely quiet workplace and those who were well adapted to (not bothered by) a noisy workplace. But when a worker complains about noise, he's telling you he doesn't fit into either of those fortunate subsets. He's telling you that he is likely to be defect-prone. You ignore that message at your peril.

A Discovery of Nobel Prize Significance

Some days, people are just more highly perceptive than other days. For us, a landmark day for perceptiveness was February 3, 1984, when we began to notice a remarkable relationship between people density and dedicated floor space per person. As the one goes up, the other seems to go down! Careful researchers that we are, we immediately began to document the trend. In a study of 32,346 companies throughout the Free World, we confirmed a virtually perfect inverse relationship between the two (see Figure 9–2).

Imagine our excitement as the data points were collected. We experienced some of the thrill that Ohm must have felt when discovering his law. This was

Figure 9-2   The DeMarco/Lister Effect.

truly the stuff of which Nobel Prizes are made. Remember that you saw it here first: Worker density (say, workers per thousand square feet) is inversely proportional to dedicated space per person.

If you're having trouble seeing why this matters, you're not thinking about noise. Noise is directly proportional to density, so halving the allotment of space per person can be expected to double the noise. Even if you managed to prove conclusively that a programmer could work in thirty square feet of space without being hopelessly space-bound, you still wouldn't be able to conclude that thirty square feet is adequate space. The noise in a thirty-square-foot matrix is more than three times the noise in a hundred-square-foot matrix. That could mean the difference between a plague of product defects and none at all.

Hiding Out

When the office environment is frustrating enough, people look for a place to hide out. They book the conference rooms or head for the library or wander off for coffee and just don't come back. No, they are not meeting for secret romance or plotting political coups; they are hiding out to *work*. The good news here is that your people really do need to feel the accomplishment of work completed. They will go to great extremes to make that happen. When the crunch is on, people will try to find workable space no matter where.

In my college years at Brown University, the trick for getting through the mad season when all the papers came due was to find some place quiet to work. At Brown, we had a system of carrels in the library stacks. The only acceptable interruption there was a fire alarm, and it had to be for a real fire. We got to be experts at finding out-of-the-way carrels where no one would ever think to look for us. The fifth-floor carrels of the Bio Library were my favorite, but a friend even went so far as to work in the crypt below the American Library—yes, the crypt, complete with the remains of the woman who had endowed the building. It was cool, it was marble, and as my friend reported, it was quiet, very quiet.

—TRL

If you peek into a conference room, you may find three people working in silence. If you wander to the cafeteria midafternoon, you're likely to find folks seated, one to a table, with their work spread out before them. Some of your workers can't be found at all. People are hiding out to get some work done. If this rings true to your organization, it's an indictment. Saving money on space may be costing you a fortune.

Intermezzo:
Productivity Measurement and
Unidentified Flying Objects

> An intermezzo is a fanciful digression inserted between the pages
> of an otherwise serious work (oh, well, fairly serious work).

Why can't we just measure productivity in good and bad workplaces
and finally nail down the relationship between the environment
and worker effectiveness? That approach would certainly be suit-
able for an assembly line, but when the work being measured is of a more
intellectual nature, it's not so obvious. Measurement of intellect-worker productivity suffers from a reputation of being a soft science. In some people's
minds, it's little better than the study of unidentified flying objects.

An experiment to test the effect of the workplace on productivity is easy
enough to design:

- Measure the amount of work completed in the new workplace.

- Measure the cost of doing that work.

- Compare the size and cost in the new workplace to the size and cost in
  the old.

Design was easy, the implementation is harder: For instance, how do you
assess the amount of work involved in a market study or in a new circuit design or in the development of a new loan policy? There may be some emerging standards (as there are in the software industry, for instance), but these
are sure to require extensive local data collection and the building of in-house
expertise. Most organizations don't even attempt to measure the amount of
intellect work performed. They don't measure costs very effectively, either.

There may be statistics on the total *quantity* of hours applied to a given
problem within an organization, but no indication of the *quality* of these
hours (more about this in Chapter 10, "Brain Time versus Body Time"). And

even if organizations could measure size and cost in a new workplace, they would have no past figures to compare them to. Managers are likely to furrow their brows over this problem, sigh, and conclude that variation in productivity is beyond comprehension. But it's really not as bad as that.

Gilb's Law

In London for one year's International Conference on Software Engineering, I spent an afternoon with Tom Gilb, the author of *Software Metrics* and dozens of published papers on measurement of the development process. I found that an easy way to get him heated up was to suggest that something you need to know is "unmeasurable." The man was offended by the very idea. He favored me that day with a description of what he considered a fundamental truth about measurability. The idea seemed at once so wise and so encouraging that I copied it verbatim into my journal under the heading of Gilb's Law:

> *Anything you need to quantify can be measured in some way that is superior to not measuring it at all.*

Gilb's Law doesn't promise you that measurement will be free or even cheap, and it may not be perfect—just better than nothing.

—TDM

Of course it's possible to measure productivity. If you convoke a group of people doing the same or similar work and give them a day to work out a sensible self-measurement scheme, they will come up with something that confirms Gilb's Law. The numbers they then generate will give them some way to tune their own performance and, when combined with quality circles or some other peer-review mechanism, a way to learn from each other's methods. The averages computed over the group will give management a reliable indicator of the effect of such parameters as improvement in the office environment.

In the field that we know best, software construction, there are any number of workable productivity measurement schemes. There are even services that will come in and assess your productivity and show you where you stand compared to the rest of the industry. An organization that can't make some assessment of its own productivity rate just hasn't tried hard enough.

But You Can't Afford Not to Know

Suppose there were a foolproof productivity measurement tool and it was being applied to your people's work this very moment. Suppose the measurers came in to tell you that your productivity was in the top 5 percent of organizations doing your kind of work. You'd be pleased. You'd wander around the halls with a secret smile, thinking warm thoughts about your people: "I suspected they were pretty good, but this is terrific news."

Ooops. The measurers have just come back to tell you that they must have been holding the graph upside down when they gave you the first report. You're actually in the bottom 5 percent. Now your day is ruined. You find yourself thinking, "I might have known it all along. Who could expect to get any work done with turkeys like these on the staff?" In the one case you're ecstatic, in the other despondent. *But in neither case are you particularly surprised.* You're not likely to be surprised no matter what the news is, because you haven't the foggiest idea what your productivity is.

Given that there are ten to one differences from one organization to another, you simply can't afford to remain ignorant of where you stand. Your competition may be ten times more effective than you are in doing the same work. If you don't know it, you can't begin to do something about it. Only the market will understand. It will take steps of its own to rectify the situation, steps that do not bode well for you.

Measuring with Your Eyes Closed

Work measurement can be a useful tool for method improvement, motivation, and enhanced job satisfaction, but it is almost never used for these purposes. Measurement schemes tend to become threatening and burdensome.

In order to make the concept deliver on its potential, management has to be perceptive and secure enough to cut itself out of the loop. That means the data on individuals is not passed up to management, and everybody in the organization knows it. Data collected on the individual's performance has to be used only to benefit that individual. The measurement scheme is an exercise in self-assessment, and only the sanitized averages are made available to the boss.

This concept is a hard one to swallow for many managers. They reason that they could use the data to do some aspects of their work more effectively (precision promotion, for example, or even precision firing). Their company has paid to have the data collected, so why shouldn't it be made available to them? But collection of this very sensitive data on the individual can only be effected with the active and willing cooperation of the individual. If ever its confidentiality is compromised, if ever the data is used against even one individual, the entire data collection scheme will come to an abrupt halt.

The individuals are inclined to do exactly the same things with the data that the manager would do. They will try to improve the things they do less well or try to specialize in the areas where they already excel. In the extreme case, an individual may even "fire" himself in order to stop depending on skills that have been found to be deficient. The manager doesn't really need the individual data in order to benefit from it.

10

Brain Time versus Body Time

As part of the Santa Teresa pre-construction study described in Chapter 9, "Saving Money on Space," McCue and his associates looked into the amounts of time that developers spend in different work modes. For a typical day, they concluded that workers divide their time as shown in Table 10-1.

The significance of this table from a noise standpoint should be evident: Thirty percent of the time, people are noise sensitive, and the rest of the time, they are noise generators. Since the workplace is a mixture of people working alone and people working together, there is a clash of modes. Those working alone are particularly inconvenienced by this clash. Though they represent a minority at any given time, it's a mistake to ignore them, for it is during their solitary work periods that people actually do the work. The rest of the time is dedicated to subsidiary activities, rest, and chatter.

Flow

During single-minded work time, people are ideally in a state that psychologists call *flow*. Flow is a condition of deep, nearly meditative involvement. In this state, there is a gentle sense of euphoria, and one is largely unaware

TABLE 10-1   How Developers Spend Their Time

Work Mode	Percent of Time
Working alone	30%
Working with one other person	50%
Working with two or more people	20%

of the passage of time: "I began to work. I looked up, and three hours had passed." There is no consciousness of effort; the work just seems to, well, flow. You've been in this state often, so we don't have to describe it to you.

Not all work roles require that you attain a state of flow in order to be productive, but for anyone involved in engineering, design, development, writing, or like tasks, flow is a must. These are high-momentum tasks. It's only when you're in flow that the work goes well.

Unfortunately, you can't turn on flow like a switch. It takes a slow descent into the subject, requiring 15 minutes or more of concentration before the state is locked in. During this immersion period, you are particularly sensitive to noise and interruption. A disruptive environment can make it difficult or impossible to attain flow.

Once locked in, the state can be broken by an interruption that is focused on you (your phone, for instance) or by insistent noise ("Attention! Paging Paul Portulaca. Will Paul Portulaca please call extension . . ."). Each time you're interrupted, you require an additional immersion period to get back into flow. During this immersion, you're not really doing work.

An Endless State of No-Flow

If the average incoming phone call takes five minutes and your reimmersion period is fifteen minutes, the total cost of that call in flow time (work time) lost is twenty minutes. A dozen phone calls use up half a day. A dozen other interruptions and the rest of the workday is gone. This is what guarantees, "You never get anything done around here between 9 and 5."

Just as important as the loss of effective time is the accompanying frustration. The worker who tries and tries to get into flow and is interrupted each time is not a happy person. He gets tantalizingly close to involvement only to be bounced back into awareness of his surroundings. Instead of the deep mindfulness that he craves, he is continually channeled into the promiscuous changing of direction that the modern office tries to force upon him. Put yourself in the position of the participant who filled out her Coding War Games time sheet with the entries shown in Table 10-2.

A few days like that and anybody is ready to look for a new job. If you're a manager, you may be relatively unsympathetic to the frustrations of being in no-flow. After all, you do most of your own work in interrupt mode—that's management—but the people who work for you need to get into flow. Anything that keeps them from it will reduce their effectiveness and the satisfaction they take in their work. It will also increase the cost of getting the work done.

TABLE 10-2 Segment of a CWG Time Sheet

Work Period From–To	Type of Work	What Interruption Caused the End of This Work Period?
2:13–2:17	Coding	Phone call
2:20–2:23	Coding	Boss stopped in to chat
2:26–2:29	Coding	Question from colleague
2:31–2:39	Coding	Phone call
2:41–2:44	Coding	Phone call

Time Accounting Based on Flow

Chances are, your company's present time-accounting system is based on a conventional model. It assumes that work accomplished is proportional to the number of paid hours put in. When workers fill out their time sheets in this scheme, they make no distinction between hours spent doing meaningful work and hours of pure frustration. So they're reporting body time rather than brain time.

To make matters worse, the task-accounting data is also used for payroll purposes. This compels employees to make sure that the total number of hours logged always balances out to some predetermined total for the week, regardless of how much overtime or undertime they put in. The resultant compilation of official fictions may be acceptable to the Payroll Department: It is equivalent to the worker responding "Present" to a roll call. But for any productivity assessment or analysis of where the money went, this record is too badly tainted to be useful.

The phenomena of flow and immersion give us a more realistic way to model how time is applied to a development task. What matters is not the amount of time you're *present,* but the amount of time that you're *working at full potential.* An hour in flow really accomplishes something, but 10 six-minute work periods sandwiched between 11 interruptions won't accomplish anything.

The mechanics of a flow-accounting system are not very complex. Instead of logging hours, people log *uninterrupted* hours. In order to get honest data, you have to remove the onus from logging too few uninterrupted hours. People have to be assured that it's not their fault if they can only manage one or two uninterrupted hours a week; rather it's the organization's fault for not providing a flow-conducive environment. Of course, none of this data can go to the Payroll Department. You'll still have to retain some body-present time-reporting for payroll purposes.

A task-accounting scheme that records flow hours instead of body-present hours can give you two huge benefits: First, it focuses your people's attention on the importance of flow time. If they learn that each workday is expected to afford them at least two or three hours free from interruption, they will take steps to protect those hours. The resultant *interrupt-consciousness* helps to protect them from casual interruption by peers.

Second, it creates a record of how meaningful time is applied to the work. If a product is projected to require three thousand flow hours to complete, then you've got a valid reason to believe you're two-thirds done when two thousand flow hours have been logged against it. That kind of analysis would be foolish and dangerous with body-present hours.

The E-Factor

If you buy the idea that a good environment ought to afford workers the possibility of working in flow, the collection of uninterrupted-hour data can give you some meaningful metric evidence of just how good or bad your environment is. Whenever the number of uninterrupted hours is a reasonably high proportion of total hours, up to approximately 40 percent, then the environment is allowing people to get into flow when they need to. Much lower numbers imply frustration and reduced effectiveness. We call this metric the *Environmental Factor* or *E-Factor:*

E-Factor = Uninterrupted Hours/Body-Present Hours

A somewhat surprising result of collecting E-Factor data is that factors vary within an organization from site to site. For example, we recorded E-Factors as high as 0.38 and as low as 0.10 in one large government agency. The agency's head assured us that the physical environment had to remain as it was, no matter how bad, because characteristics of the workplace were determined by government policy and by civil service level. In spite of this, we found some sites where workers were housed in a tight, noisy open-office plan, and others where workers doing the same job and at the same level worked in pleasant four-person offices. Not so surprising was the finding that E-Factors were markedly higher in the four-person offices.

E-Factors can be threatening to the status quo. (Perhaps you'd better not even start collecting the data.) If you report 0.38 for a sensible space and 0.10 for a cost-reduced space, for example, people are likely to conclude that the cost reduction didn't make much sense. Workers in the 0.10 space will have to put in 3.8 times as much body-present time to do a given piece of work as those in the 0.38 space. That means having work done in the cost-reduced space could result in a performance penalty that is far greater than the space savings. Clearly, such a heretical line of reasoning must be suppressed. Otherwise we jeopardize all those wonderful "savings" to be gained by tightening up your workers' spaces. Burn this book before anyone else sees it.

A Garden of Bandannas

When you first start measuring the E-Factor, don't be surprised if it hovers around zero. People may even laugh at you for trying to record uninterrupted hours: "There is no such thing as an uninterrupted hour in this madhouse." Don't despair. Remember that you're not just collecting data, you're helping to change people's attitudes. By regularly noting uninterrupted hours, you are giving official sanction to the notion that people ought to have at least some interrupt-free time. That makes it permissible to hide out, to ignore the phone, or to close the door (if, sigh, there is a door).

At one of our client sites, there was a nearly organic phenomenon of red bandannas on dowels suddenly sprouting from the desks after a few weeks of E-Factor data collection. No one in power had ever suggested that device as an official Do Not Disturb signal; it just happened by consensus. But everyone soon learned its significance and respected it.

Of course, there have always been certain cranky souls who have stuck up Do Not Disturb signs. Peer pressure makes it hard for most of us to show that interruptions aren't welcome, even for a part of the day. A little emphasis on the E-Factor helps to change the corporate culture and make it acceptable to be uninterruptable.

Thinking on the Job

In my years at Bell Labs, we worked in two-person offices. They were spacious, quiet, and the phones could be diverted. I shared my office with Wendl Thomis, who went on to build a small empire as an electronic toy maker. In those days, he was working on the Electronic Switching System fault dictionary. The dictionary scheme relied upon the notion of n-space proximity, a concept that was hairy enough to challenge even Wendl's powers of concentration. One afternoon, I was bent over a program listing while Wendl was staring into space, his feet propped up on the desk. Our boss came in and asked, "Wendl! What are you doing?" Wendl said, "I'm thinking." And the boss said, "Can't you do that at home?"

—TDM

The difference between that Bell Labs environment and a typical modern-day office plan is that in those quiet offices, one at least had the option of thinking on the job. In most of the office space we encounter today, there is enough noise and interruption to make any serious thinking virtually impossible. More is the shame: Your people bring their brains with them every morning. They could put them to work for you at no additional cost if only there were a small measure of peace and quiet in the workplace.

11

The Telephone

When you begin to collect data about the quality of work time, your attention is automatically focused on one of the principal causes of interruption, the incoming telephone call. It's nothing to field 15 calls in a day. It may be nothing, but because of the associated reimmersion time, it can use up most of that day. When the day is over and you're wondering where the time went, you can seldom even remember who called you or why. Even if some of the calls were important, they may not have been worth interrupting your flow. But who's got the nerves to wait out a ringing phone? The very thought of it makes you tense between the shoulders.

Visit to an Alternate Reality

Now just relax and imagine a less complicated world in which the phone has not yet been invented. In such a world, you write a note to propose lunch or a meeting and you get a note in response. Everyone plans ahead a little bit more. It's common to take half an hour in the morning to read and answer your mail. There are no loud bells in your life.

Wednesday mornings in this alternate reality are dedicated to meetings of your company's pension trust investment committee. Imagine for the moment you are one of the employee representatives charged with watching where the money is placed. On this particular Wednesday, an inventor is scheduled to make a presentation to the committee. The inventor has plans to change the world, if only you'll invest in his new contraption. His name is A.G. Bell.

"Ladies and Gentlemen, this is the BellOPhone!" (The man unwraps a large black box with a crank on the side and an enormous bell attached to the top.)

"This is the future. We're going to put one of these on every desk in America. Homes, too! It will get to the point where people can hardly imagine a world without them."

As he warms up to his subject, he begins gesticulating enthusiastically and hopping around the room to make his points. "BellOPhones everywhere you look, all of them hooked up together with wires under the street or overhead. And now this is the really exciting part: You can get your BellOPhone specifically connected to somebody else's BellOPhone, even though it may be all the way across the city or maybe in some other city. And when you've connected it just by entering the code, you can make the bell ring on the other fellow's machine. Not just some rinky-dink bell, either, but a real heart-stopper."

He sets up a second device and connects it to the first, on the other side of the room. By manipulating a dial on the face of the first, he causes the other machine to come alive. It gives off a loud BBRRRRIINNNGGGG! After half a second, it rings again and then again and again, deafeningly.

"Now, what's a fellow got to do to stop this ringing? He's got to race over to his BellOPhone and pick up the receiver." He picks up the receiver on the ringing device and hands it to one of the committee members. Then he bounds back to the other side of the room and starts shouting into the mouthpiece of the originating device. "'Hello! Hello! Can you hear me?' See that, I've got his complete attention. Now I can sell him something, or get him to lend me money or try to change his religion or whatever I want!"

The committee is stunned. You raise your hand and venture a question, "Since nobody could possibly have missed the first ring, why bother to repeat it?"

"Ah, that's the beauty of the BellOPhone," says A.G. "It never gives you the chance to wonder whether you want to answer it or not. No matter what you're involved in at the time it rings, no matter how engrossed you are, you drop everything to answer it. Otherwise, you know it will just keep on ringing. We're going to sell billions of these things and never ever allow any to be sold that rings only once."

The committee goes into a huddle, but it doesn't take very long to come up with a judgment. You all decide without a dissenting voice to throw this turkey out the door. The device is so disruptive that if you were ever dumb enough to allow it to be installed, nobody would ever get any work done around the office. A few years' effect of the BellOPhone and we'd all be reduced to buying goods from Taiwan and Korea. And our country might even have a negative balance of trade.

Tales from the Crypt

Of course, there's no turning the calendar back. The telephone is here to stay. You can't get rid of it, nor would you probably want to. You certainly can't remove phones from people's desks without causing them to revolt. But there are certain steps that can be taken to minimize the negative impact of interruptive calls. The most important of these is to realize how much we have allowed the telephone to dominate our time allocation.

Do you often interrupt a discussion with co-workers or friends to answer a phone? Of course you do. You don't even consider not answering the phone. Yet what you're doing is a violation of the common rules of fairness, taking people out of order, just because they insist loudly (BBRRRRIINNNGGGG!) on your attention. Not only do you do this to others, you let them do it to you. And you're so inured to this abuse that you hardly take note of it. Only in the most outrageous cases is it clear that something is definitely wrong with such behavior.

Back in my twenties, I was standing in line at the parts department of the New York dealer for Morgan Motorcars Limited. I had a nonfunctioning Morgan (the only kind) and was hoping to get some new carburetor needles. People who drive British sports cars are undoubtedly masochists, but the treatment in that parts line was just too much. The clerk took one phone call after another while everyone in line waited. When I got to the head of the line, he took four calls in quick succession before I could get in a single word. I began thinking, Why should people calling from the comfort of their homes get priority over those of us standing here in this stupid line? Why should those mere window shoppers be taken ahead of customers with money in their hands, ready to buy? In a state of pure red rage, I suggested that he let the phone ring for a while and take people ahead of bells. To my surprise, he was more annoyed by my behavior than I was by his. He informed me very huffily that phones get priority over people, and that was all there was to it. My not liking it was as pointless as not liking the Atlantic Ocean. The facts of life weren't going to change just to suit me.

—TDM

It is natural that the telephone should have reshaped somewhat the way we do business, but it ought not to have blinded us to the effects of the interruptions. At the least, managers ought to be alert to the effect that interruption can have on their own people who are trying to get something done. But often it's the manager who is the worst offender. One of the programmers in the 1985 Coding War Games wrote on his environmental survey, "When my boss is out, he has his calls switched to me." What could that manager have been thinking? What was going on in the mind of the systems department head who wrote this in a memo:

> *It has come to my attention that many of you, when you are busy, are letting your phones ring for three rings and thus get switched over to one of the secretaries. With all these interruptions, the secretaries can never get any productive work done. The official policy here is that when you're at your desk you will answer your phone before the third ring. . . .*

A Modified Telephone Ethic

Enough is enough. The path toward sanity in working conditions is a new attitude toward interruptions and toward the telephone. People who are charged with getting work done must have some peace and quiet to do it in. That means periods of total freedom from interruptions. When they want to work in flow, they have to have some efficient, acceptable way of ignoring incoming calls. "Acceptable" means the corporate culture realizes that people may sometimes choose to be unavailable for interruption by phone. "Efficient" means that they don't have to wait out the bell in order to get back to work.

There are workable schemes to help people free themselves from phones and other interruptions when they find it necessary. (Some of these cost money, and thus will be possible only in organizations whose long-term view extends beyond next Tuesday.)

When electronic mail was first proposed, most of us thought that the great value of it would be the saving in paper. That turns out to be trivial, however, compared to the saving in reimmersion time. The big difference between a phone call and an electronic mail message is that the phone call interrupts and the e-mail does not; the receiver deals with it at his or her own convenience. The amount of productive traffic going through these systems proves that priority "at the receiver's convenience" is acceptable for the great majority of business communications. After a period of acclimatization, workers begin to use electronic mail in preference to intra-company calls. It doesn't make all the calls go away, only most.

Most of us now have perfectly acceptable voice-mail and e-mail. The trick isn't in the technology; it is in the changing of habits. (Gentle reader, please note this recurring theme.) We have to learn to ask, Does this kind of news or question deserve an interrupt? Can I continue to get work done while I wait for an answer? Does this message need immediate recognition? If not, how long can it wait without causing a problem?

Once you ask these questions, your best mode of communication is usually pretty obvious.

Incompatible Multitasking

When you're doing think-intensive work like design, interruptions are productivity killers. When you're also doing sales and marketing support for the product you and your colleagues are designing, then you have to take every single call that comes in. Same with user support for another product.

To the extent that knowledge workers are required to multitask, their managers need to take account of the flow requirements of the different tasks. Mixing flow and highly interruptive activities is a recipe for nothing but frustration. In particular, it assures that no reasonable telephone ethic ("Leave me alone. I'm working.") can emerge.

More important than any gimmick you introduce is a change in attitude. People must learn that it's okay sometimes not to answer their phones, and their managers need to understand that as well. That's the character of knowledge workers' work: The quality of their time is important, not just its quantity.

A cursory reading of this chapter might leave you thinking that the entire message is,

telephone: bad; e-mail: good

but it's a bit more complicated than that. More on this subject in Chapter 33, "E(vil) Mail."

12

Bring Back the Door

There are some prevalent symbols of success and failure in creating a sensible workplace. The most obvious symbol of success is the door. When there are sufficient doors, workers can control noise and interruptibility to suit their changing needs. The most obvious symbol of failure is the paging system. Organizations that regularly interrupt everyone to locate one person are showing themselves to be totally insensitive to the imperatives of a work-conducive environment.

Manipulate these symbols and you not only call attention to your concern for a workable environment, you also reap the immediate associated advantage: People can get on with the work. But it sounds like a tall order, to get rid of the paging system and bring back the door. Is it beyond our capacity to effect these changes?

The Show Isn't Over Till the Fat Lady Sings

The degradation of working conditions that has affected most of us over the past decades has depended on the consent of the victim. That doesn't mean that one such victim could have halted the trend by saying, "No, I won't work in noisy, cramped, exposed space." But it does mean that we as a group haven't hollered loud enough and often enough about the counterproductive side effects of saving money on space.

While most of us believed that the trend toward noisier, tighter space was hurting productivity, we kept silent, because we lacked the definitive statistical evidence that proved our case. The Furniture Police, of course, didn't provide any proof at all to support their contention that people would be just as productive working cheek-by-jowl as they had been in a more sensible environment. They just asserted that it was true.

We need to learn from them, learn to fight fire with fire. So, the first step toward a sane environment is a program of repeated assertion. If you believe that the environment is working against you, you've got to start saying so. You'll need to create a forum for other people to chime in, too, perhaps with a survey of people's assessment of their working conditions. (In one such survey at a client company, workers cited seven negative aspects of their work, things they thought of as productivity-limiters. Of these, the first four were noise-related.)

As people begin to realize that they aren't alone in their feelings, environmental awareness increases. And with this increased awareness, two good things begin to happen: First, the environment improves a bit as people try to be more thoughtful about noise and interruption; and second, the consent of the victim is withdrawn. It now becomes harder for upper management to take any other step to improve productivity without first paying some attention to the environment.

Don't expect the Establishment to roll over and play dead just because you begin your campaign. There are (at least) three counterarguments bound to surface almost immediately:

- People don't care about glitzy office space. They're too intelligent for that. And the ones who do care are just playing status games.

- Maybe noise is a problem, but there are cheaper ways to deal with it than mucking around with the physical layout. We could just pipe in white noise or Muzak and cover up the disturbance.

- Enclosed offices don't make for a vital environment. We want people to interact productively, and that's what they want, too. So walls and doors would be a step in the wrong direction.

We deal with these objections in the next three subsections.

The Issue of Glitz

It's true that people don't care much about glitz. In one study after another, workers failed to give much weight to decor in choosing, for instance, among variously colored panels and fixtures. The feeling seemed to be that depressing surroundings would be counterproductive, but as long as the office wasn't depressing, then you could happily ignore it and get down to work. If all we're shooting for is an ignorable workplace, then money spent on high-fashion decor is a waste.

The fact that workers don't care a lot about appearances is often misinterpreted to mean that they don't care a lot about any of the attributes of the workplace. If you ask them specifically about noise, privacy, and table and counter space, though, you'll hear some strongly felt opinions that these characteristics matter a lot. This finding is consistent with the idea of an ignorable workplace as ideal; one can't ignore a workplace that is forever interrupting, paging, and generally harassing the worker.

We find it particularly distressing to hear workers' concerns about their environment dismissed as status-seeking, because it's more often the case that higher management is guilty of status-seeking in designing the workers' space. The person who is working hard to deliver a high-quality product on time is not concerned with office appearances, but the boss sometimes is. So we see the paradoxical phenomenon that totally unworkable space is gussied up expensively and pointlessly with plush carpets, black and chrome furniture, corn plants that get more space than workers, and elaborate panels. The next time someone proudly shows you around a newly designed office, think hard about whether it's the functionality of the space that is being touted or its appearance. All too often, it's the appearance.

Appearance is stressed far too much in workplace design. What is more relevant is whether the workplace lets you work or inhibits you. Work-conducive office space is not a status symbol, it's a necessity. Either you pay for it by shelling out what it costs, or you pay for it in lost productivity.

Creative Space

In response to workers' gripes about noise, you can either treat the symptom or treat the cause. Treating the cause means choosing isolation in the form of noise barriers—walls and doors—and these cost money. Treating the symptom is much cheaper. When you install Muzak or some other form of pink noise, the disruptive noise is drowned out at small expense. You can save even more money by ignoring the problem altogether so that people have to resort to iPods and headphones to protect themselves from the noise. If you take either of these approaches, you should expect to incur an invisible penalty in one aspect of workers' performance: They will be less creative.

During the 1960s, researchers at Cornell University conducted a series of tests on the effects of working with music. They polled a group of computer science students and divided the students into two groups, those who liked to have music in the background while they worked (studied) and those who did not. Then they put half of each group together in a silent room, and the other half of each group in a different room equipped with earphones and a musical selection. Participants in both rooms were given a programming problem to work out from specification. To no one's surprise, participants in the two rooms performed about the same in speed and accuracy of programming. As any kid who does his arithmetic homework with the music on knows, the part of the brain required for arithmetic and related logic is unbothered by music— there's another brain center that listens to the music.

The Cornell experiment, however, contained a hidden wild card. The specification required that an output data stream be formed through a series of manipulations on numbers in the input data stream. For example, participants had to shift each number two digits to the left and then divide by one hundred and so on, perhaps completing a dozen operations in total. Although the specification never said it, the net effect of all the operations was that each output number was necessarily equal to its input number. Some people realized this and others did not. Of those who figured it out, the overwhelming majority came from the quiet room.

Many of the everyday tasks performed by professional workers are done in the serial processing center of the left brain. Music will not interfere particularly with this work, since it's the brain's holistic right side that digests music. But not all of the work is centered in the left brain. There is that occasional breakthrough that makes you say "Ahah!" and steers you toward an ingenious bypass that may save months or years of work. The creative leap involves right-brain function. If the right brain is busy listening to "1,001 Strings" on Muzak, the opportunity for a creative leap is lost.

The creativity penalty exacted by the environment is insidious. Since creativity is a sometime thing anyway, we often don't notice when there is less of it. People don't have a quota for creative thoughts. The effect of reduced creativity is cumulative over a long period. The organization is less effective, people grind out the work without a spark of excitement, and the best people leave.

Vital Space

The case against enclosed offices sooner or later gets around to the "sterility" of working alone. But enclosed offices need not be one-person offices. The two- or three- or four-person office makes a lot more sense, particularly if office groupings can be made to align with work groups. The worker who needs to spend 50 percent of his time with one other person will spend most of that time with a particular person. These two are natural candidates to share an office.

Even in open-plan offices, co-workers should be encouraged to modify the grid to put their areas together into small suites. When this is allowed, people become positively ingenious in laying out the area to serve all their needs: work space, meeting space, and social space. Since they tend to be in interaction mode together or simultaneously in flow mode, they have less noise clash with each other than they would with randomly selected neighbors. The space has a vital quality because interaction is easy and natural. A degree of control over their space is viewed as an additional benefit.

Breaking the Corporate Mold

What could be less threatening than a proposal to allow people to reorganize open-plan seating into shared suites instead of individual cubicles? One of the great benefits of the kind of "office system" (that is, no offices) that your company may have purchased is its flexibility. At least that's what the EZ-Whammo Panel System brochure says. So it should be easy enough to move things around. Letting people form suites may seem non-threatening, but we predict that someone in the upper reaches of the organization will hate the idea. The problem is that the hallowed principle of uniformity is violated. By making everything uniform, the "owner" of a territory exercises and demonstrates control. Like the gardener who plants seeds exactly under a taut string so that the carrots will grow in a perfect row, this manager is threatened by the kind of minor disorder that nature (in this case, people's human nature) prefers.

The inconvenient fact of life is that the best workplace is not going to be infinitely replicable. Vital work-conducive space for one person is not exactly the same as that for someone else. If you let them, your people will make their space into whatever they need it to be and the result is that it won't be uniform. Each person's space and each team's space will have a definite character of its own. If it didn't, they'd go back and alter it until it did.

Management, at its best, should make sure there is enough space, enough quiet, and enough ways to ensure privacy so that people can create their own sensible work space. Uniformity has no place in this view. You have to grin and bear it when people put up odd pictures or clutter their desks or move the furniture around or merge their offices. When they've got it just the way they want it, they'll be able to put it out of their minds entirely and get on with the work.

13

Taking Umbrella Steps

For this final chapter on the office environment, we look into characteristics of an ideal workplace, trying to shed some light on concerns such as these:

- What kind of space would support your workers best to make them comfortable, happy, and productive?
- What form of work space would make these workers feel best about themselves and about their work?

If you work in a typical, noisy, and dreadfully uniform corporate space, such questions may seem almost cruel. But thinking about ideal space is worthwhile. Someday, you may be in a position to make it happen. Even today, you may be called upon to provide some input to the process of work-space improvement. It's sensible to indulge yourself a bit on the subject of space, just to know where you ought to be headed. Where you ought to be headed, in our opinion, is toward a work space that has certain time-proven characteristics.

There is one timeless way of building.

It is thousands of years old, and the same today as it has always been.

The great traditional buildings of the past, the villages and tents and temples in which man feels at home, have always been made by people who were very close to the center of this way. It is not possible to make great buildings, or great towns, beautiful places,

> *places where you feel yourself, places where you feel alive, except*
> *by following this way. And, as you will see, this way will lead*
> *anyone who looks for it to buildings which are themselves as an-*
> *cient in their form, as the trees and hills, and as our faces are.*
>
> —Christopher Alexander, *The Timeless Way of Building*[1]

Christopher Alexander, architect and philosopher, is best known for his observations on the design process. He frames his concepts in an architectural idiom, but some of his ideas have had influence far beyond the field of architecture. (Alexander's book *Notes on the Synthesis of Form*, for example, is considered a kind of holy book by designers of all kinds.) Together with his colleagues at the Center for Environmental Structure, Alexander set out to codify the elements of good architectural design. The resultant work is a three-volume set entitled *The Timeless Way of Building*. The effect of this work is still being debated. Alexander believes that most modern architecture is bankrupt, and so most modern architects are understandably a bit defensive about the man and his ideas. But when you hold these books in your own hands and examine their premises against your own experience, it's hard not to take Alexander's side. His philosophy of interior space is a compelling one. It helps you to understand what it is that has made you love certain spaces and never feel comfortable in others.

Alexander's Concept of Organic Order

Imagine that your organization is about to build a complex of new space. What is the first step in this process? Almost certainly, it is development of a master plan. In most cases, this is a first and fatal deviation from *The Timeless Way of Building*. Vital, exciting, and harmonious spaces are never developed this way. The master plan envisions hugeness and grandeur, steel and concrete spans, modular approaches and replication to make an enormous whole of identical components. The result is sterile uniformity and space that doesn't work for anyone except the one Ego to whom it stands as a tribute.

Most monolithic corporate space can only be understood in terms of its symbolic value to the executives who caused it to be built. This is their mark on the firmament, the lasting accomplishment they leave behind. They gloat, "Look on my works, ye Mighty, and despair!" Despair, of course, is exactly all you can do. Your cubicle, infinitely repeated to the horizon, leaves you feeling like a numbered cog. Whether it is TransAmerica's Orwellian tower in San

---

1. *The Timeless Way of Building* by Christopher Alexander (1979): 106 words (p. 7) © 1979 by Christopher Alexander. "By Permission of Oxford University Press."

Francisco or AT&T's Madison Avenue mausoleum, the result is depressingly the same: a sense of suffocation to the individual.

The master plan is an attempt to impose totalitarian order. A single and therefore uniform vision governs the whole. In no two places is the same function achieved differently. A side effect of the totalitarian view is that the conceptualization of the facility is frozen in time.

In place of the master plan, Alexander proposes a meta-plan. It is a philosophy by which a facility can grow in an evolutionary fashion to achieve the needs of its occupants. The meta-plan has three parts:

- A philosophy of piecemeal growth

- A set of patterns or shared design principles governing growth

- Local control of design by those who will occupy the space

Under the meta-plan, facilities evolve through a series of small steps into campuses and communities of related buildings. By respecting the shared principles, they retain a harmony of vision, but not a sameness. Like mature villages, they begin to take on an evolved charm. This is what Alexander calls *organic order,* as described below and as shown in Figure 13-1.

> *This natural or organic order emerges when there is perfect balance between the needs of the individual parts of the environment, and the needs of the whole. In an organic environment, every place is unique and the different places also cooperate, with no parts left over, to create a global whole—a whole which can be identified by everyone who is a part of it.*
>
> *The University of Cambridge is a perfect example of organic order. One of the most beautiful features of this university is the way the colleges—St. Johns, Trinity, Trinity Hall, Clare, Kings, Peterhouse, Queens—lie between the main street of the town and the river. Each college is a system of residential courts, each college has its entrance on the street, and opens onto the river; each college has its own small bridge that crosses the river, and leads to the meadows beyond; each college has its own boathouse and its own walks along the river. But while each college repeats the same system, each one has its own unique character. The individual courts, entrances, bridges, boathouses and walks are all different.*
>
> *—Christopher Alexander, The Oregon Experiment*[2]

---

2. *The Oregon Experiment* by Christopher Alexander et al. (1975): 188 words (pp. 10–11) © 1975 by Christopher Alexander. "By Permission of Oxford University Press."

Figure 13-1 Swiss town, an example of organic order, without a master plan.[3]

Patterns

Each of the patterns of *The Timeless Way of Building* is an abstraction about successful space and interior order. The central volume of the set, *A Pattern Language*, presents 253 of these patterns and weaves them into a coherent view of architecture. Some of the patterns have to do with light and roominess, others with decor, or with the relationship between interior and exterior space, or with space for adults, for children, for elders, or with traffic movement around and through enclosed space. Each pattern is presented as a simple architectural aphorism, together with a picture that illustrates it and a lesson. In between, there is a discussion of the whys and wherefores of the pattern. As an example, consider the following illustration and extract from Pattern 183, Workspace Enclosure:

> *People cannot work effectively if their workspace is too enclosed or too exposed. A good workspace strikes the balance. . . . You feel more comfortable in a workspace if there is a wall behind you. . . . There should be no blank wall closer than eight feet in front of you. (As you work, you want to occasionally look up and rest your eyes by focusing them on something farther away than the desk. If there*

---

3. Ibid., p. 46.

Figure 13-2 Workspace enclosure.[4]

is a blank wall closer than eight feet your eyes will not change fo-cus and they get no relief. In this case you feel too enclosed.) . . . You should not be able to hear noises very different from the kind you make, from your workplace. Your workplace should be suf-ficiently enclosed to cut out noises which are a different kind from the ones you make. There is some evidence that one can concen-trate on a task better if people around him are doing the same thing, not something else. . . . Workspaces should allow you to face in different directions.

—Christopher Alexander, A Pattern Language[5]

To complement the 253 basic patterns, teams need to prepare a set of new patterns tailored to the specific nature of their project. For the purposes of the next four subsections, we have nominated ourselves to be one such team. Our charter is to design sensible work space for people who make their living

---

4. *A Pattern Language* by Christopher Alexander et al. (1977): 170 words (p. 846) © 1977 by Christopher Alexander. "By Permission of Oxford University Press."
5. Ibid., pp. 847–51.

by thinking. The four patterns we propose take aim at four of the worst failings of present-day institutional space. In forming these patterns, we borrow heavily from those of our clients that have succeeded in creating successful workplaces.

The First Pattern: Tailored Work Space from a Kit

Today's modular cubicle is a masterpiece of compromise: It gives you no meaningful privacy and yet still manages to make you feel isolated. You are poorly protected from noise and disruption; indeed in some cases, sources of noise and disruption are actively piped into your space. You're isolated because that small lonely space excludes everyone but you (it's kind of a toilet stall without a toilet). The space makes it difficult to work alone and almost impossible to participate in the social unit that might form around your work.

Individual modules give poor-quality space to the person working alone and no space at all to the team. The alternative to this is to fashion space explicitly around the working groups. Each team needs identifiable public and semiprivate space. Each individual needs protected private space.

Groups of people who have been assigned or have elected to work together need to have a meaningful role in the design of their own space. Ideally, they are aided in this by a central space-planning organization, whose job is to find a chunk of space for the group: "I see there are three of you, so you'll be needing three hundred square feet or more. Yes, here's a nice possibility. Now let's think about layout and furniture. . . ." The team members and their space counselor next begin to work out the possible ways their space could be arranged (see Figure 13–3).

Because of the requirement that workers be allowed to participate in the design of their own space, whatever system of desks and fixtures the company uses has to perform in a truly modular fashion. Instead of fitting only into a simple grid, the furnishings must be useful in myriad different configurations.

The Second Pattern: Windows

Modern office politics makes a great class distinction in the matter of allocating windows. Most participants emerge as losers in the window sweepstakes. People who wouldn't think of living in a home without windows end up

Figure 13–3   Possible space arrangements.

spending most of their daylight time in windowless work space. Alexander has very little patience with windowless space: "Rooms without a view are like prisons for the people who have to stay in them."

We are trained to accept windowless office space as inevitable. The company would love for every one of us to have a window, we hear, but that just isn't realistic. Sure it is. There is a perfect proof that sufficient windows can be built into a space without excessive cost. The existence proof is the hotel, any hotel. You can't even imagine being shown a hotel room with no window. You wouldn't stand for it. (And this is for a space you're only going to sleep in.) So hotels are constructed with lots of windows.

Figure 13–4   Women's dormitory at Swarthmore College.[6]

The problem of windowless space is a direct result of a square aspect ratio. If buildings are constructed in a fairly narrow shape, there need be no shortage of windows. A sensible limit for building width is thirty feet, such as the building shown in Figure 13–4.

Limit buildings to thirty feet in width? Can this be a serious proposal? What about costs? What about the economies of scale that come with building enormous indoor spaces? Some years ago, the Danish legislature passed a law that every worker must have his or her own window. This law has forced builders to construct long, narrow buildings, planned along the lines of hotels and apartment buildings. In studies conducted after the law had been in effect for a while, there was no very noticeable change in cost of space per square meter. That doesn't mean the narrow configuration had no cost significance, only that the increase, if any, was too small to show up in the data. Even if there is a higher cost per worker to house people in the more agreeable space, the added expense is likely to make good sense because of the savings it provides in other areas. The real problem is that the cost is in a highly visible category (space and services), while the offsetting advantage is in poorly measured and therefore invisible categories (increased productivity and reduced turnover).

6. *The Oregon Experiment* by Christopher Alexander et al. (1975): 188 words (p. 125) © 1975 by Christopher Alexander. "By Permission of Oxford University Press."

The Third Pattern: Indoor and Outdoor Space

The narrow configuration also makes it possible to achieve greater integration between indoor and outdoor space. If you've ever had the opportunity to work in space that had an outdoor component, it's hard to imagine ever again limiting yourself to working entirely indoors.

Upon formation of The Atlantic Systems Guild in 1983, we set out to find Manhattan space to serve as a guild hall and office for New York-based members. The space we found was the top floor of a Greenwich Village ship chandlery. It consisted of two-thousand square feet indoors and a thousand-square-foot outdoor terrace. The terrace became our spring, summer, and fall conference room and eating area. For at least half the year, the outdoor space was in use virtually full-time. Whatever work could be done outdoors was done outdoors.

Before you dismiss our solution as an impossible luxury, think about this fact: We paid less than a third as much per square foot as the Manhattan average. Our space cost a lot less because it was not part of a monolith. You can't accommodate thousands of people centrally in such space. You'd have to hunt out hundreds of special situations in order to get a large staff into anything like the situation we came up with. And when you did that, they would not all have identical facilities. On a given sunny day, some of your people would be working on terraces while others were in gardens or arbors or courtyards. How un-uniform.

The Fourth Pattern: Public Space

An age-old pattern of interior space is one that has a smooth "intimacy gradient" as you move toward the interior. At the extremity is space where outsiders (messengers and tradesmen and salesmen) may penetrate. Then you move into space that is reserved for insiders (the work group or the family), and finally to space that is only for the individual. This pattern applies to your home as you move from foyer to living room to kitchen to bedroom to bathroom. And it should be true as well of a healthy workplace.

At the entrance to the workplace should be some area that belongs to the whole group. It constitutes a kind of hearth for the group. Further along the intimacy gradient should be space for the tightly knit work groups to interact and to socialize. Finally, there is the protected quiet thinking space for one person to work alone.

Group interaction space needs tables and seating for the whole group, writing surfaces, and areas to post whatever group members want to post. Ideally, there should also be a space for members to prepare simple meals and eat together:

> *Without communal eating, no human group can hold together. Give each [working group] a place where people can eat together. Make the common meal a regular event. In particular, start a common lunch in every workplace so that a genuine meal around a common table (not out of boxes, machines or bags) becomes an important, comfortable and daily event. . . . In our own work group at the Center, we found this worked most beautifully when we took it in turns to cook the lunch. The lunch became an event: a gathering: something that each of us put our love and energy into.*
>
> *—Christopher Alexander, A Pattern Language[7]*

The Pattern of the Patterns

The patterns that crop up again and again in successful space are there because they are in fundamental accord with characteristics of the human creature. They allow him to function as a human. They emphasize his essence—he is at once an individual and a member of a group. They deny neither his individuality nor his inclination to bond into teams. They let him be what he is.

A common element that runs through all the patterns (both ours and Alexander's) is *reliance upon non-replicable formulas.* No two people have to have exactly the same work space. No two coffee areas have to be identical, nor any two libraries or sitting areas. The texture and shape and organization of space are fascinating issues to the people who occupy that space. The space needs to be isomorphic to the work that goes on there. And people at all levels need to leave their mark on the workplace.

Return to Reality

Now, what does all this have to do with you? If you work for a large institution, you're not likely to convince the powers that be to admit the error of their ways and allow everyone to build a Timeless-Way sort of workplace.

---

7. *A Pattern Language* by Christopher Alexander et al. (1977): 170 words (pp. 697–99) © 1977 by Christopher Alexander. "By Permission of Oxford University Press."

And perhaps you don't want to work for a small company in which charming and idiosyncratic workplaces occur rather naturally.

There is nonetheless a possible way to put your people into vital, productive space. The possibility arises because master-planned space is almost always full, and it's a continual hassle to find a place to house any new effort. If you run one of those as-yet-unhoused efforts, turn your sights outward. Petition to move your group out of the corporate monolith. You may be turned down, but then again, since there's no space for you in-house, you may not. Put your people to work to find and arrange their own space. Never mind that it may not have the same white plastic wastebaskets or corduroy-covered partitions as the headquarters' space. If you can pick up a lease on a run-down fraternity house or garden apartment that would make cheap, idiosyncratic, fascinating quarters for your people, well then, so what that they will be housed differently from everyone else in the company? If it's okay with them, who cares?

You don't have to solve the space problem for the whole institution. If you can solve it just for your own people, you're way ahead. And if your group is more productive and has lower turnover, that just proves you're a better manager.

It almost always makes sense to move a project or work group out of corporate space. Work conducted in ad hoc space has got more energy and a higher success rate. People suffer less from noise and interruption and frustration. The quirky nature of their space helps them form a group identity. If you are part of the lofty reaches of upper management, then decide which projects matter most. Move the key ones out. It's a sad comment that an important piece of work is likely to fare better off-site. It's sad but true. Make it work for you.

PART III

The Right People

The final outcome of any effort is more a function of *who* does the work than of *how* the work is done. Yet modern management science pays almost no attention to hiring and keeping the right people. Any management course you're likely to take barely gives lip service to these aspects.

Management science is much more concerned with the boss's role as principal strategist and tactician of the work. You are taught to think of management as playing out one of those battle simulation board games. There are no personalities or individual talents to be reckoned with in such a game; you succeed or fail based on your decisions of when and where to deploy your faceless resources.

In the next four chapters, we will attempt to undo the damage of the manager-as-strategist view, and replace it with an approach that encourages you to court success with this formula:

- Get the right people.

- Make them happy so they don't want to leave.

- Turn them loose.

Of course, you have to coordinate the efforts of even the best team so that all the individual contributions add up to an integrated whole. But that's the relatively mechanical part of management. For most efforts, success or failure is in the cards from the moment the team is formed and the initial directions set out. With talented people, the manager can almost coast from that point on.

14

The Hornblower Factor

C. S. Forester's series of novels on the Napoleonic Wars follows the exploits of Horatio Hornblower, an officer in England's Royal Navy. On one level, these are pure adventure stories set in a well-researched historical framework. On another level, the Hornblower books can be read as an elaborate management analogy. The job of running a square-rigged frigate or ship of the line is not so different from that of managing a project or a company division. The tasks of staffing, training, work allocation, scheduling, and tactical support will be familiar to anyone involved in management today.

Hornblower is the ultimate manager. His career advanced from midshipman to admiral through the same blend of cleverness, daring, political maneuvering, and good luck that has promoted any of the corporate high-fliers featured in the pages of *Business Week*. There is a real-world management lesson to be learned from his every decision.

Born versus Made

A recurrent theme through all the novels is Hornblower's gloomy presentiment that achievers are born, not made. Many of the subordinates that fall to him through luck of the draw are undependable or stupid. He knows that they all will let him down at some key moment. (They always do.) He also knows that the few good men who come his way are his only real resource. Sizing them up quickly and knowing when to depend on them are Hornblower's great talents.

In our egalitarian times, it's almost unthinkable to write someone off as intrinsically incompetent. There is supposed to be inherent worth in every human being. Managers are supposed to use their leadership skills to bring out untapped qualities in each subordinate. This shaping of raw human material is considered the essence of management.

That view may be more comforting than Hornblower's glum assessment, and it certainly is more flattering to managers, but it doesn't seem very realistic to us. Parents do have a shaping effect on their children over the years, and individuals can obviously bring about huge changes in themselves. But managers are unlikely to change their people in any meaningful way. People usually don't stay put long enough, and the manager just doesn't have enough leverage to make a difference in their nature. So the people who work for you through whatever period will be more or less the same at the end as they were at the beginning. If they're not right for the job from the start, they never will be.

All of this means that getting the right people in the first place is all-important. Fortunately, you don't have to depend entirely on the luck of the draw. You may get to play a significant part in the hiring of new people or the selection of new team members from within the company. If so, your skill at these tasks will determine to a large extent your eventual success.

The Uniform Plastic Person

Even novice managers, setting out to hire staff for the first time, know something about the principles of good hiring. They know, for instance, that you can't hire based on appearance. The best-looking candidate is not one whit more likely to deliver a good product than a candidate who is homely.

Everybody knows that, but oddly enough most hiring mistakes result from too much attention to appearances and not enough to capabilities. This is not just due to ignorance or shallowness on the part of the person doing the hiring. Evolution has planted in each of us a certain uneasiness toward people who differ by very much from the norm. It is clear how this tendency serves evolution's purposes. You can observe this evolutionary defense in yourself in your reactions to a horror film, for instance. The almost human "creature" is much more upsetting than the mile-wide eyeless blob that slowly digests Detroit.

As each individual matures, he or she learns to override the built-in bias toward the norm in selecting friends and developing close relationships. Though you may have learned that lesson long ago in your personal life, you have to learn it all over again as you develop your hiring skills.

You probably don't feel that you have an uncontrollable tendency to hire attractive or "normal" looking people. So why are we talking about this at all?

Because it's not just your individual tendency toward the norm that affects your hiring, it's also your organization's subliminal imposition of a norm of its own. Each person you hire becomes part of your little empire and also part of your boss's empire and that of the next boss up the line. The standard you apply is not just your own. You're hiring on behalf of the whole corporate ladder above you. The perceived norm of these upper managers is working on you each time you consider making a new offer. That almost unsensed pressure is pushing toward the company average, encouraging you to hire people that look like, sound like, and think like everybody else. In a healthy corporate culture, this effect can be small enough to ignore. But when the culture is unhealthy, it's difficult or impossible to hire the one person who matters most, the one who doesn't think like all the rest.

The need for uniformity is a sign of insecurity on the part of management. Strong managers don't care when team members cut their hair or whether they wear ties. Their pride is tied only to their staff's accomplishments.

Standard Dress

Uniformity is so important to insecure authoritarian regimes (parochial schools and armies, for example) that they even impose dress codes. Different lengths of skirt or colors of jacket are threatening, and so they are forbidden. Nothing is allowed to mar the long rows of nearly identical troops. Accomplishment matters only to the extent it can be achieved by people who don't look different.

Companies, too, sometimes impose standards of dress. These are not so extreme as to oblige strictly uniform attire, but they remove considerable discretion from the individual. When this first happens, the effect is devastating. People can talk and think of nothing else. All useful work stops dead. The most valuable people begin to realize that they aren't appreciated for their real worth, that their contributions to the work are not as important as their haircuts and neckties. Eventually they leave. And the rest of the company plods on, trying to prove that having the right people wasn't so important after all.

Throughout these pages, we've suggested remedies for some of the things that can go wrong in organizations. But if what's gone wrong in yours is promulgation of a formal standard of appearance, forget it. It's too late for a remedy. The organization is suffering from the last stages of brain death. The corpse won't topple over immediately, since there are so many hands trying to prop it up. But propping up corpses is unsatisfying work. Get yourself a new job.

Code Word: *Professional*

When I alluded to management insecurity as the cause of arbitrary standardization, participants at one in-house seminar could barely restrain themselves. They all had stories to tell. One of the silliest had to do with the company's reaction to use of the coffee area microwave to pop some popcorn during afternoon break. Of course, popping corn leaves an unmistakable smell. Someone from the rarified altitudes of upper management smelled the smell and reacted. He declared in a memo, "Popcorn is not professional," and so would henceforth be forbidden.

—TRL

An anti-popcorn standard or even a dress standard might be understandable if you worked in the Customer Relations Department or in Sales. But in any other area, it makes no sense at all. There is seldom if ever a client wandering through such space. These "standards" have nothing to do with the organization's image as perceived by outsiders. It's the image perceived by insiders that matters. The insiders in question—typically second- and third-level managers with shaky self-confidence—are uncomfortable with any kind of behavior that is different from average. They need to impose safely homogenized mores on those beneath them to demonstrate that they are in charge.

The term *unprofessional* is often used to characterize surprising and threatening behavior. Anything that upsets the weak manager is almost by definition unprofessional. So popcorn is unprofessional. Long hair is unprofessional if it grows out of a male head, but perfectly okay if it grows out of a female head. Posters of any kind are unprofessional. Comfortable shoes are unprofessional. Dancing around your desk when something good happens is unprofessional. Giggling and laughing is unprofessional. (It's all right to smile, but not too often.)

Conversely, *professional* means unsurprising. You will be considered professional to the extent you look, act, and think like everyone else, a perfect drone.

Of course, this perverted sense of professionalism is pathological. In a healthier organizational culture, people are thought professional to the extent they are knowledgeable and competent.

Corporate Entropy

Entropy is levelness or sameness. The more it increases, the less potential there is to generate energy or do work. In the corporation or other organization, entropy can be thought of as uniformity of attitude, appearance, and thought process. Just as thermodynamic entropy is always increasing in the universe, so, too, corporate entropy is on the rise:

SECOND THERMODYNAMIC LAW OF MANAGEMENT:
Entropy is always increasing in the organization.

That's why most elderly institutions are tighter and a lot less fun than sprightly young companies.

There is not much you can do about this as a global phenomenon, but you've got to fight it within your own domain. The most successful manager is the one who shakes up the local entropy to bring in the right people and let them be themselves, even though they may deviate from the corporate norm. Your organization may have rigor mortis, but your little piece of it can hop and skip.

15

Let's Talk about Leadership

L eadership on the job is rare, but talk about it is ubiquitous. Companies talk about it all the time.

The talk is usually about the adroit exercise of organizational power to accomplish a given end. It's managers who lead. Managers are sent off to leadership training to enable them to better use their authority to direct those who work for them. In this view, leadership is something that happens *down* the hierarchy—leaders at the top, followers at the bottom. You are led by the person who is above you on the org. chart and you lead those whose boxes on the chart lie under yours with lines directly down from your box.

Leadership as a Work-Extraction Mechanism

One of those dreadful "motivational" posters tells us, "The speed of the leader sets the rate of the pack." This kind of leadership is a work-extraction mechanism. Its purpose is to enhance not the *quality* of the experience but the *quantity*. The reason you are being led is to get you to work harder, stay longer, and stop goofing off.

During the early part of the First World War, a young Russian journalist named Lev Davidovich Bronstein wrote home from the front with some observations about leadership. His letters might have been lost, but since he later became the revolutionary Trotsky, they are preserved. In one letter he observes that unless they are given side arms, the junior officers will be completely unable to lead their men into battle. Using a gun to lead means you have to "lead" from behind. This is what work-extraction leadership is all about. The gun, in the workplace, is replaced with delegated authority and positional power.

Leadership as a Service

But the best leadership—the kind that people can mention only with evident emotion and deep respect—is most often exercised by people without positional power. It happens outside the official hierarchy of delegated authority.

When I'm on my home turf, I play tennis two or three times a week in groups organized by a charming fellow named Mike. Mike is our leader. It's Mike who decides the matchups: who plays with whom and against whom. He's the one who shuffles the players (16 of us on four courts) after each set so we all have different partners for all three sets. He invariably makes good pairings so that near the end of a half hour you can look across the courts and see four scores like 5 to 4, 6 to 6, 7 to 6, and 5 to 5. He has a great booming voice, easy to hear even when he is three courts away. He sets the meeting times, negotiates the schedules for court time, and makes sure there are subs for anyone who needs to be away. Nobody gave Mike the job of leading the group; he just stepped up and took it. His leadership is uncontested; the rest of us are just in awe of our good fortune that he leads us as he does. He gets nothing for it except our gratitude and esteem.

—TDM

In this example, leadership is not about extracting anything from us; it's about service. The leadership that the Mikes of the world provide enables their endeavors to go forth. While they sometimes set explicit directions, their main role is that of a catalyst, not a director. They make it possible for the magic to happen.

In order to lead without positional authority—without anyone ever appointing you leader—you have to do what Mike does:

- Step up to the task.

- Be evidently fit for the task.

- Prepare for the task by doing the required homework ahead of time.

- Maximize value to everyone.

- Do it all with humor and obvious goodwill.

It also helps to have charisma.

Leadership and Innovation

The propensity to lead without being given the authority to do so is what, in organizations, distinguishes people that can innovate and break free of the constraints that limit their competitors. Innovation is all about leadership, and leadership is all about innovation. The rarity of the one is a direct result of the rarity of the other.

Innovation is a subject whose talk:do ratio is even more out of whack than that of leadership. Upper management in most companies talks a good game on innovation. The party line goes something like this: "We need innovation to survive. It is so important. Its importance simply cannot be overstated. No sir. Innovation is reeealy, reeealy important. And innovation is everybody's job. In fact, it is probably the most important part of everybody's job. Listen up, everybody: Get out there and innovate." Oh, and by the way,

- Nobody is given any time to innovate, since everyone is 100-percent busy.

- Most innovation that happens anyway is distinctly unwelcome because it requires accommodating change.

- Real innovation is likely to spread beyond the realm of the innovator, and so he or she may be suspected of managing the organization from below, a tendency that upper management tends to view with great suspicion.

The net here is that it takes a bit of a rebel to help even the best innovation achieve its promise: rebel leadership. The innovator himself doesn't have to be a great leader, but someone has to be. What rebel leadership supplies to this process is the time to innovate—you take a key person away from doing billable work (this may constitute constructive disobedience on your part) in order to pursue a nascent vision—and the hard push for whatever reshaping the organization has to submit to in order to take advantage of the innovation.

Since nobody ever knows how the next innovation may alter the organization, nobody knows enough to give permission to the key instigators to do what needs to be done. That's why leadership as a service almost always operates without official permission.

Leadership: The Talk and the Do

At a recent Broadway performance of Arthur Miller's *Death of a Salesman*, I was struck by a line that comes near the end of the final act. The protagonist, Willy Loman, approaches his well-to-do neighbor, Charley, to ask for yet another small loan. The sad contrast between Charley's fortunes and Willy's own failure is reflected in their sons: Willy's son Biff has gone badly downhill, while Charley's son, Bernard, has become a successful lawyer. Charley makes the loan and tells Willy proudly that Bernard is off to Washington, D.C., to argue a case before the Supreme Court. Imagine that, the United States Supreme Court.

> *"The Supreme Court!" Willy says. "And he didn't even mention it!"*
>
> *"He don't have to—" Charley replies, "he's gonna do it."*

—TRL

If companies were more inclined to let leadership arise naturally, they wouldn't need to produce so much hot air talking about it.

16
Hiring a Juggler

Circus Manager: How long have you been juggling?

Candidate: Oh, about six years.

Manager: Can you handle three balls, four balls, and five balls?

Candidate: Yes, yes, and yes.

Manager: Do you work with flaming objects?

Candidate: Sure.

Manager: . . . knives, axes, open cigar boxes, floppy hats?

Candidate: I can juggle anything.

Manager: Do you have a line of funny patter that goes with your juggling?

Candidate: It's hilarious.

Manager: Well, that sounds fine. I guess you're hired.

Candidate: Umm . . . Don't you want to see me juggle?

Manager: Gee, I never thought of that.

It would be ludicrous to think of hiring a juggler without first seeing him perform. That's just common sense. Yet when you set out to hire an engineer or a designer or a programmer or a group manager, the rules of common sense are often suspended. You don't ask to see a design or a program or anything. In fact, the interview is just talk.

You're hiring a person to produce a product, presumably similar to those he or she has made before. You need to examine a sample of those products to see the quality of work the candidate does. That may seem obvious, but it's almost always overlooked by development managers. There is a surface reserve at work when you meet for a job interview. There seems to be an unwritten rule that says it's okay to ask the candidate about past work but not to ask to see it. Yet when you ask, candidates are almost always pleased to bring along a sample.

The Portfolio

During one of our joint teaching gigs in western Canada, we got a call from a computer science professor at the local technical college. He proposed to stop by our hotel after class one evening and buy us beers in exchange for ideas. That's the kind of offer we seldom turn down. What we learned from him that evening was almost certainly worth more than whatever he learned from us.

The teacher was candid about what he needed to be judged a success in his work: He needed his students to get good job offers and lots of them. "A Harvard diploma is worth something in and of itself, but our diploma isn't worth squat. If this year's graduates don't get hired fast, there are no students next year and I'm out of a job." So he had developed a formula to make his graduates optimally attractive to the job market. Of course, he taught them a diversity of modern techniques for system construction. He also had them work on real applications for nearby companies and agencies. But the center-piece of his formula was the portfolio that all students put together to show samples of their work.

He described how his students had been coached to show off their portfolios as part of each interview:

> I've brought along some samples of the kind of work I do. Here, for instance, is a subroutine in C++ from one project and a set of SAP scripts from another. As you can see in this portion, we use the loop-with-exit extension advocated by Knuth, but aside from that, it's pure structured code, pretty much the sort of thing that your company standard calls for. And here is the design that this code was written from. And these are the leveled data flow diagrams that make up the guts of our specification, and the associated data dictionary. . . .

In the years since, we've often heard more about that obscure technical college and those portfolios. We've met recruiters from as far away as Triangle Park, North Carolina, and Tampa, Florida, who regularly converge upon that distant Canadian campus for a shot at its graduates.

Of course, this was a clever scheme of the professor's to give added allure to his graduates, but what struck us most that evening was the report that interviewers were always surprised by the portfolios. That meant they weren't regularly requiring all candidates to arrive with portfolios. Yet why not? What could be more sensible than asking each candidate to bring along some samples of work to the interview?

Aptitude Tests (Erghhhh)

If it's so important that the new hire be good at the various skills used in the job, why not design an aptitude test to measure those skills? Our industry has had a long, irregular flirtation with the idea of aptitude testing. In the sixties, the idea was positively in vogue. By now, you and your organization have probably given up on the concept. In case you haven't, we offer one good reason that you ought to: The tests measure the wrong thing.

Aptitude tests are almost always oriented toward the tasks the person will perform immediately after being hired. They test whether he or she is likely to be good at statistical analysis or programming or whatever it is that's required in the position. You can buy aptitude tests in virtually any technical area, and they all tend to have fairly respectable track records at predicting how well the new hire will perform. But so what? A successful new hire might do those tasks for a few years and then move on to be team leader or a product manager or a project head. That person might end up doing the tasks that the test measured for two years and then do other things for twenty.

The aptitude tests we've seen are mostly left-brain oriented. That's because the typical things new hires do are performed largely in the left brain. The things they do later on in their career, however, are to a much greater degree right-brain activities. Management, in particular, requires holistic thinking, heuristic judgment, and intuition based upon experience. So the aptitude test may give you people who perform better in the short term, but are less likely to succeed later on. Maybe you should use an aptitude test but hire only those who fail it.

From your reading of this book, you'd hardly expect its authors to endorse the idea of hiring through the use of aptitude tests. But it doesn't follow that aptitude tests are no good or that you ought not to be using them. You should use them, just not for hiring. The typical aptitude test you buy or build can be a wonderful self-assessment vehicle for your people. Frequent interesting opportunities for private self-assessment are a must for workers in a healthy organization. (More about this in Chapter 37, "Chaos and Order.")

Holding an Audition

The business we're in is more sociological than technological, more dependent on workers' abilities to communicate with each other than their abilities to communicate with machines. So the hiring process needs to focus on at least some sociological and human communication traits. The best way we've discovered to do this is through the use of auditions for job candidates.

The idea is simple enough. You ask a candidate to prepare a ten- or fifteen-minute presentation on some aspect of past work. It could be about a new technology and the experience with first trying it out, or about a management lesson learned the hard way, or about a particularly interesting project. The candidate chooses the subject. The date is set and you assemble a small audience made up of those who will be the new hire's co-workers.

Of course, the candidate will be nervous, perhaps even reluctant to undertake such an experience. You'll have to explain that all candidates are nervous about the audition and give your reasons for holding one: to see the various candidates' communication skills, and to give the future co-workers a part in the hiring process.

At the end of the audition and after the candidate has left, you hold a debriefing of those present. Each one gets to comment on the person's suitability for the job and whether he or she seems likely to fit well into the team. Although it's ultimately your responsibility to decide whether to hire or not, the feedback from future co-workers can be invaluable. Even more important, any new person hired is more likely to be accepted smoothly into the group, since the other group members have had a voice in choosing the candidate.

My first experience with auditions was in hiring people to be consultants and instructors. My motivation in torturing these prospective hires was simple enough: I wanted to get a sense of whether they were natural explainers of matters simple or complex, or people who could be taught to explain such matters, or those who could never explain anything to anyone. I also wanted some second opinions on the matter, so I had those of my people who were in the office at the time of the audition sit in on the presentation. Over five years, we conducted nearly two hundred auditions.

It soon became clear that the audition process served to accelerate the socialization process between a new hire and the existing staff members. A successful audition was a kind of certification as a peer. The reverse seemed to hold true as well. Failed auditions were a morale booster for the staff. They were continuing proof that being hired for the group was more than just the dumb luck of when résumés happened to hit my desk.

—TRL

One caveat about auditions: Make sure the candidate speaks about something immediately germane to the work your organization does. It's easy to be snookered by a talk on a topic from extreme left field, like "Elder Care for Triplets" or "Effects of Soft Drinks on Turnip Growth." You're liable to catch a glimpse of a very compelling passion on the speaker's part, a passion that you'll never see again on the job.

17

Playing Well with Others

ontractors, outsourcers, and offshore personnel add an extra dimension to the problem of reasonable team formation. In addition, the internationalization of practically everything means that even the most plain-vanilla, in-house team can oblige you to try to knit together team members from widely different origins. The "class picture" you take of your next project team is likely to show something that looks more like a United Nations task force than the kind of single-culture group that our fathers and grandfathers managed. Melding the mix into a team can be a challenge, but there are benefits as well.

First, the Benefits

Old guys like us can remember a day when technology teams tended to have no women, or almost no women. The software industry, in the U.S. at least, was the catalyst for an exploding female workforce. In *Software Engineering Economics,* Barry Boehm points out that the industry grew from essentially zero billion dollars a year to thirty billion dollars a year in just over 25 years. Most of that money was people-cost. And where did all those people come from? They couldn't come from the same sources that were supplying the other high-tech industries because those sectors were themselves growing. They couldn't be the other obvious choices coming out of the university systems—male math and computer science majors—because there simply weren't enough of them. The key was to tap into the untapped resource of educated women whose earlier career choices had been severely limited. The hiring companies had to teach specific skills like programming and debugging

109

and systems design to these women, but they'd have had to teach those same skills to newly graduated male hires anyway, since few universities during most of the period that Boehm studied were offering useful software skills courses to their students.

Women brought much more to their new industry than just labor hours. They changed the way that teams were organized and how team members interacted. They complemented our tired old sports analogies with new images from ballet, child rearing, and family dynamics. As they moved into management, they introduced new styles, what our colleague Sheila Brady calls "seat of the skirt management." Today, an all-male team seems thin and less than totally energized. Women made a huge difference.

Food Magic

The breakdown of borders through globalization and common markets brought new kinds of diversity, more nationalities, and new cultural patterns to our projects. If these changes have seemed like a bother to accommodate, they also brought richness. Think about cuisine: Most probably, your great-grandparents never encountered a market offering Chinese dumplings, Bombay lime pickle, lemongrass curry, tiramisu, and gnocci, but these foods are now an integral part of the modern world. (If you were transported back a century in time, you might find much to amuse you, but you would probably be bored to tears by your dinner choices.) We don't hide the differences in cuisines; we relish them.

One of the teams I work with started a "Bring in an Ethnic Dish for Lunch" event once a month, and it was such a hit that it soon became twice a month. Each dish was something a bit exotic, prepared by team members with different backgrounds.

—TRL

Just as we relish the different foods diverse members may bring to the table, so too we need to relish the different ways they tend to work and think and communicate.

Yes, But . . .

That said, the capacity of a team to absorb newness has its limits. Twenty contractors this month, three the next month, and fifteen the third month means you have just had to integrate 38 new people during your project. You need extra planning to avoid renting humans like you rent cars.

Team jell takes time, and, during much of that time, the composition of the team can't be changing. If you need to use a reactive strategy of contract labor, your team will probably never jell. In fact, the workforce you manage almost certainly won't be a team at all.

18
Childhood's End

In Arthur C. Clarke's science-fiction epic *Childhood's End*, the tension derives from a new generation of humans that are not just quantitatively, but qualitatively different from their parents. The significance of the title is that the arrival of this generation marks childhood's end for the human species. Evolution has played a nasty trick on the parents, making them suddenly the new Neanderthals, while their children become *homo superbus*.

Young people arriving in the workplace today are not quite *that* different, but there are some generational differences that need to be understood and accommodated.

Technology—and Its Opposite

Disney Fellow Alan Kay defines *technology* as whatever is around you today but was not there when you were growing up. He further observes that what was already around you when you were growing up has a name: It's called *environment*. One generation's technology is the next generation's environment.

There was some important technology in the workplace at the end of the twentieth century that was not yet ubiquitous in homes and schools. That is much less true today. For your youngest employees, computers, smart phones, the Web, programming, hacking, social networking, and blogging are environment, not technology. You can't teach them much about the mechanics of these matters, and anything you have to say about the associated ethics for their use is all too likely to fall on deaf ears. And yet, if they're to progress from new kids in the company to valued employees, you and they are going to have to come to some understanding on the proper uses of your technology/environment.

Continuous Partial Attention

In the most-simplistic terms, the new generational divide in your organization is about attention: Young people divide theirs while their older colleagues tend to focus on one or possibly two tasks at a time.

A generation that grew up studying with music blaring on their iPods, text messages flooding in and out, social networking sites open at all hours, and a video game going on sporadically in a window beside the history assignment is an illustration of what former Microsoft Vice President Linda Stone has called "continuous partial attention." Your youngest hires will tell you that they operate most effectively in this environment.

The problem is that continuous partial attention is the exact opposite of flow. If you believe, as we do, that a flow state is essential for getting real work done, then you need to set limits on how attention may be divided. You need to make your youngest workers understand the difference between spending 2 percent of their workday on Facebook *in a single block of time* and spending 2 percent of their attention *all day* on Facebook. The one may be a reasonable accommodation for human workers' personal needs (much like the occasional call or text message home during working hours), while the other may be a deterrent to their ever fitting in. Workers who can't get into flow are not just less effective, they also are unlikely to fit into a jelled team of mixed-generation people.

Articulate the Contract

My first boss, Lee Toumenoska at Bell Labs, took me aside on Day One and said, "Look, Tom, here's the deal: We work here from eight forty-five until five-fifteen, with an hour off for lunch. That makes a seven-and-a-half-hour workday, thirty-seven and a half hours per week. That's what you get paid for. I want you to respect those hours. If you absolutely need to be late, be an hour or two late, not five minutes one day and then ten the next, and so on, until you're not pulling the same as everyone else." I needed to be told that. I had no idea what the contract was—what did I know, a 22-year-old who'd never had a real job before?

—TDM

Articulating the contract to young workers is going to be essential to give them a chance to fit in. If work needs to be done in flow, then your people need to be ready to focus. Continuous-partial-attention periods have to be defined as personal time off, acceptable within limits during the workday. The rest of the workday is for, well, work.

Continuous partial attention at meetings is similarly destructive of whatever the legitimate purposes may be of the meeting. But if yours is like other companies we visit, this is not solely a generational problem. Even your older workers may be prone to doing e-mail and other tasks during meetings. Think of imperfect attention at meetings to be more about a dysfunctional meeting culture than about anyone's work ethic. Stand-up meetings and meetings without open laptops are a way to articulate the contract, but expect such a move to require you to rethink your meeting philosophy, almost certainly a good idea. (More about this in Chapter 31, "Meetings, Monologues, and Conversations.")

Yesterday's Killer App

Your youngest workers are not going to arrive at the door with much regard for e-mail. If you've thought of e-mail, as we have, as definitive of the modern world, then get ready for a shock.

For the last few years, I've been teaching an undergraduate ethics course at the University of Maine. It's a writing course, and so I have tried to impress upon my students the value and necessity of iteration from draft to draft. In a typical assignment, I asked them to submit a first draft to me on a given Friday with a second draft due the next Friday. Then I worked over the weekend to mark up their first drafts, and sent them back via e-mail. To my surprise, almost none of my students took into account my mark-ups in preparing their second drafts. I asked why and learned that essentially none of them ever looked at their e-mail. They suggested that I text them if I had placed something they'd need to look at in their In-boxes.

—TDM

The younger your people are, the more likely they are to see e-mail as a verbose and dreary waste of time. The terseness of texting is much more to their taste. In an era that celebrates bandwidth, the hot technology for them is the lowest bandwidth tool available: typing with their thumbs.

(If our dystopian perspective in Chapter 33, "E(vil) Mail," leaves you sputtering, don't hire any young workers.)

19

Happy to Be Here

This chapter begins with a pop quiz:

Q1: What annual employee turnover has your organization experienced over the last few years?

Q2: How much does it cost on average to replace a person who leaves?

Score yourself as follows: If you had any answer at all to the two questions, you pass. Otherwise, you fail. Most people fail.

In all fairness, perhaps it's not your job to know about such things. Okay, we'll re-score your quiz. You pass if *anyone* in your organization has a real answer to the two questions. Most people still fail. We avoid measuring turnover for the same reason that heavy smokers avoid having long serious talks with their doctors about longevity: It's a lot of bother that can only result in bad news.

Turnover: The Obvious Costs

Typical turnover figures we encounter are in the range of 80 percent to 33 percent per year, implying an average employee longevity of from 15 to 36 months. Assume for the moment that the turnover for your company is in the middle of this range. The average person leaves after a little more than two years. It costs one-and-a-half to two months' salary to hire a new employee, either as a fee to an agency, or as the cost of an in-house personnel service that does the same function. The employee, once hired, may go right to work on a project, in which case his or her hours are all billed to the project—there is no indication of start-up cost. This is, however, a pure book-keeping fiction. We all know that a new employee is quite useless on Day One or even worse than useless, since someone else's time is required to begin bringing the new person up to speed.

By the end of a few months, the new person is doing some useful work; within five months, he or she is at full working capacity. A reasonable assess-ment of start-up cost is therefore approximately three lost work-months per new hire. (Obviously, the start-up cost is worse or much worse to the extent that the work to be performed is highly esoteric.) The total cost of replacing each person is the equivalent of four-and-a-half to five months of employee cost or about 20 percent of the cost of keeping that employee for the full two years on the job.

Turnover varies enormously from one organization to another. We hear of companies with a 10-percent turnover, and others in the same business with 100-percent or higher turnover. At any chance gathering of managers from rival companies, you can expect that the person seated next to you has got a turnover rate that is different from yours by more than a factor of two. Of course, neither of you knows which way this difference works, and you never will because at least one of the two of you probably works for a company that doesn't measure turnover.

The Hidden Costs of Turnover

Employee turnover costs about 20 percent of all manpower expense. But that's only the *visible* cost of turnover. There is an ugly invisible cost that can be far worse.

In companies with high turnover, people tend toward a destructively short-term viewpoint, because they know they just aren't going to be there very long. So if you find yourself campaigning for better work space for your staff, for example, don't be surprised to bump into someone up the hierarchy who counters with an argument like this:

> *Hold on there, Buster. You're talking about big bucks. If we gave our engineers that much space and noise protection and even privacy, we might end up spending fifty dollars per person per month! Multiply that times all the engineers and you're into the tens of thousands of dollars. We can't spend that kind of money. I'm as much in favor of productivity as the next guy, but have you seen what a terrible third quarter we're having?*

Of course, the irrevocably logical answer to this is that investing now in a sensible environment will help to avoid terrible third quarters in the future. But save your breath. You have encountered a short-term perspective that no amount of irrevocable logic is going to sway. This person is on his or her way out of the company. The short-term cost is very real, but the long-term benefit has no meaning whatsoever.

In an organization with high turnover, nobody is willing to take the long view. If the organization is a bank, it will lend money to the Ugandan Development Corporation because the 22-percent interest looks terrific on this quarter's books. Of course, the UDC may default in a couple of years, but who's even going to be here then? If the organization is a development shop, it will optimize for the short term, exploit people, cheat on the workplace, and do nothing to conserve its very lifeblood, the peopleware that is its only real asset. If we ran our agricultural economy on the same basis, we'd eat our seed corn immediately and all starve next year.

If people only stick around a year or two, the only way to conserve the best people is to promote them quickly. That means near beginners being promoted into first-level management positions. They may have only five years of experience and perhaps less than a year with the company.

There is something very disconcerting about these numbers. A person with a work life of, say, forty years will spend five years working and thirty-five managing. That implies an exceedingly tall, narrow hierarchy. Fifteen percent of the staff is doing work, with 85 percent managing. As little as 10 percent of the cost could be spent on the workers, with 90 percent going to reward the managers. Even Marx didn't foresee such top-heaviness of capitalistic structures.

Not only is the structure wastefully top-heavy, it tends to have very lightweight people at the bottom. This is somewhat true throughout the industry, but strikingly true in high-turnover companies. It's not unusual to see serious, mature companies turning out products that are developed by workers with an average age in their twenties, and average experience of less than two years.

Many of us have come to believe that companies that promote early are where the action is. That's natural, because as young workers we're eager to get ahead. But from the corporate perspective, late promotion is a sign of health. In companies with low turnover, promotion into the first-level management position comes only after as much as ten years with the company. (This has long been true of some of the strongest organizations within IBM, for example.) The people at the lowest level have on the average at least five years' experience. The hierarchy is low and flat.

Why People Leave

For the individuals considering a change in job, the reasons can be as many and varied as the personalities involved. For the organization with pathologically high turnover (anything over 30 percent), a few reasons account for most departures:

- A just-passing-through mentality: Co-workers engender no feelings of long-term involvement in the job.

- A feeling of disposability: Management can only think of its workers as interchangeable parts (since turnover is so high, nobody is indispensable).

- A sense that loyalty would be ludicrous: Who could be loyal to an organization that views its people as parts?

The insidious effect here is that turnover engenders turnover. People leave quickly, so there's no use spending money on training. Since the company has invested nothing in the individual, the individual thinks nothing of moving on. New people are not hired for their extraordinary qualities, since replacing extraordinary qualities is too difficult. The feeling that the company sees nothing extraordinary in the worker makes the worker feel unappreciated as an individual. Other people are leaving all the time, so there's something wrong with you if you're still here next year.

A Special Pathology: The Company Move

There is no bigger ego trip for insecure managers than moving the company to some distant place. That is Wheeling and Dealing at its best! Injecting so much misery into workers' lives makes the managers feel positively god-like. The normal business of running the company lets them control their people's work lives, but the move lets them have a measure of control over even their personal lives.

Of course, they are marvelously somber when explaining the rationale behind the move. They talk about the escalating price of space or the tax structure of the old location and the benefits of the new one. Whatever the reasons given for the move, you can be sure the real reasons are very different. The real reason for the move is a political deal, or a chance to build a new edifice (finally, a piece of physical evidence of their importance), or reduction of the boss's commute by moving the company to the suburb where the boss happens to live. Sometimes it's simply the naked exercise of power.

The more egocentric the manager, the more intense the fondness for the company move. Listen to Robert Townsend on the subject:

> *If you've inherited (or built) an office that needs a real house cleaning, the only sure cure is move the whole thing out of town, leaving the dead wood behind. One of my friends has done it four times with different companies. The results are always the same: 1) The good ones are confident of their futures and go with you. 2) The people with dubious futures (and their wives) don't have to face the fact that they've been fired. "The company left town," they say. They get job offers quickly, usually from your competitors who think they're conducting a raid. 3) The new people at Destiny City are better than the ones you left behind and they're infused with enthusiasm because they've been exposed only to your best people.*[1]

What this is, to use a technical term, is the purest crap. One thing Townsend seems to have missed entirely is the presence of women in the workforce. The typical person being moved today is part of a two-career family. The other half of that equation is probably not being moved, so the corporate move comes down hard on the couple's relationship at a very delicate point. It brings intolerable stress to bear on the accommodation they're both striving to achieve to allow two full-fledged careers. That's hitting below the belt. Modern couples won't put up with it and they won't forgive it. The company move might have been possible in the 1950s and 1960s. Today it is folly.

Even in the sixties, organizational moves didn't make much sense. A case in point is the decision by AT&T's Bell Laboratories to move the 600-person ESS1 project from New Jersey to Illinois in 1966. There were many reasons given for the move, but it now seems likely that there were some political shenanigans involved. In the 1950s, then Senators Kennedy and Johnson had arranged for huge new investments in Massachusetts and Texas, and Senator Dirksen of Illinois had something coming. What a coup for Dirksen if 600 high-salary, low-pollution jobs could be moved into his state. A little pressure on AT&T, perhaps, to trade off the move against concessions in some

---

1. R. Townsend, *Up the Organization* (New York: Alfred A. Knopf, 1970), p. 64.

antitrust matter or regulatory relief. The rationale within the Labs was that the cost wouldn't be too excessive: a few thousand dollars per person in relocation expenses and maybe a bit of turnover. . . .

Years after the ESS cutover, I arranged to interview Ray Ketchledge, who had run the project. I was writing some essays on management of large efforts, and ESS certainly qualified. I asked him what he saw as his main successes and failures as boss. "Forget the successes," he said. "The failure was that move. You can't believe what it cost us in turnover." He went on to give some figures. The immediately calculable cost of the move was the number of people who quit before relocation day. Expressed as a percentage of those moved, this initial turnover was greater than the French losses in the trenches of World War I.

—TDM

You can do less damage to your organization by lining up the staff in front of a machine gun than you do by moving. And that accounts only for the initial loss. In the case of Bell Labs, there was another large exodus starting about a year after the move. These were the people who had honestly tried to go along with the company. They moved and, when they didn't like the new location, they moved again.

The Mentality of Permanence

Over the years, we have been privileged to work and consult for a few companies with extraordinarily low turnover. You won't be surprised to learn that low turnover is not the only good thing about these companies. Indeed, they seem to excel at many or most of the people-conscious qualities discussed in these pages. They are the best.

The best organizations are not of a kind; they are more notable for their dissimilarities than for their likenesses. But one thing that they all share is a preoccupation with being the best. It is a constant topic in the corridors, in working meetings, and in bull sessions. The converse of this effect is equally true: In organizations that are not "the best," the topic is rarely or never discussed.

The best organizations are consciously striving to be best. This is a common goal that provides common direction, joint satisfaction, and a strong binding effect. There is a mentality of permanence about such places, the sense that you'd be dumb to look for a job elsewhere—people would look at you as though you were daft. This is the kind of community feeling that characterized the American small towns of the past. It is something too often missing from the cities and municipalities where we live, so it is all the more important in the workplace. Some ambitious companies set out explicitly to engender a sense of community. At Reader's Digest and certain Hewlett-Packard locations, for example, the company has set up community gardens for employees. At lunch hour, the fields are full of amateur hoers and weeders and people talking tomatoes over their fences. There are contests to grow the sweetest pea or the longest zucchini, and active bartering sessions where you can trade away some of your garlic for corn.

You can prove that community gardens don't make any sense at all in the short term. Whatever costs there are will come right out of this quarter's bottom line. At most companies, that would be enough to quash the concept immediately. But in the best organizations, the short term is not the only thing that matters. What matters more is being best. And that's a long-term concept.

People tend to stay at such companies because there is a *widespread sense that you are expected to stay*. The company invests hugely in your personal growth. There may be a Master's program or an extensive training period for new hires, as much as a year in some places. It's hard to miss the message that you are expected to stay, when the company has just invested that much in your formation.

A common feature of companies with the lowest turnover is widespread retraining. You're forever bumping into managers and officers who started out as secretaries, payroll clerks, or in the mailroom. They came into the company green, often right out of school. When they needed new skills to make a change, the company provided those skills. No job is a dead end.

Again, one can prove that retraining is not the cheapest way to fill a new slot. It's always cheaper in the short run to fire the person who needs retraining and hire someone else who already has the required skills. Most organizations do just that. The best organizations do not. They realize that retraining helps to build the mentality of permanence that results in low turnover and a strong sense of community. They realize that it more than justifies its cost.

At Southern California Edison some years ago, the person in charge of all data processing began as a meter reader. At EG&G, there was a program of retraining administrative staff to become systems analysts. At the Bureau of Labor Statistics, philosophy Ph.D.s are hired to become software developers and the retraining starts with their first day on the job. At Hitachi Software, the chief scientist has as his principal function the training of new hires. At Pacific Bell, a main source of new systems people is the retrained lineman or operator. These companies are different from the norm. They feel different. There is an energy and sense of belonging that is practically palpable. It makes you feel sorry for the companies that don't have it.

20

Human Capital

Somewhere not too far from you as you read these words, there is probably a heating or air-conditioning unit in operation. Electricity and possibly some combustible fuel are working to alter the local atmosphere to keep you comfortable. These things cost money. You, or your company, pay the bill each month, annotating the charge as Utilities, or some such. Let's say that the bill for the month of September is $100, that it's paid by the company, and that the company has no other financial transaction all month: no income, no salaries, no nothing. Just one utility bill. At the end of the month, the organization's profit-and-loss statement looks like Figure 20-1.

The statement shows a loss for the month, since expenses exceeded income.

The next month is also a bit slow. Again, the company has no income and no salaries. But now the weather has warmed up, producing a month of perfect October days in which you left the windows open and never turned on

Whatever Corp.
Profit and Loss
September 2012

	Sep '12
Ordinary Income/Expense	
Expense	
Utilities	100.00
Total Expense	100.00
Net Ordinary Income	−100.00
Net Income	−100.00

Figure 20-1   P&L for the first month.

Whatever Corp.
Profit and Loss
October 2012

Oct '12

Net Income   0.00

Figure 20–2   P&L for the second month.

the heat. So, there is no utility bill to pay. You do, however, cut one check: You buy a tiny palm-top computer for $100. When you write the check, you enter it as "Computing Equipment," since that is the most obvious of the expenditure categories suggested by your accounting package. At the end of this month, your P&L looks like Figure 20–2.

Last month, your single $100 check netted against no income resulted in a loss. This month, the single check for $100 netted against no income produced a breakeven. Why the difference? The difference can only be attributed to the different categories you chose for the expenditures. In September, an expenditure for Utilities was treated as an expense; in October, an expenditure for Computing Equipment received an entirely different treatment. Your accounting package understood that Computing Equipment is just another kind of asset, like money in a different bank account. So, it treated the check like a transfer from one bank account to another. It had no effect on profit and loss.

An *expense* is money that gets used up. At the end of the month, the money is gone and so is the heat (or whatever the expense was for). An *investment,* on the other hand, is use of an asset to purchase another asset. The value has not been used up, but only converted from one form to another. When you treat an expenditure as an investment instead of as an expense, you are *capitalizing* the expenditure.

How About People?

What about money that the company spends on people? The general accounting convention is that all salaries are treated as expense, never as capital investment. Sometimes this makes sense, but sometimes it doesn't. When a worker is building a product that gets sold, it hardly matters: Whether you expense his labor or capitalize it, the amount of money paid to the worker eventually gets deducted from the sales price of the product, in order to calculate profit. You can hardly be faulted for expensing his labor the same way you expense the heat that kept the factory warm; both the labor and the heat are gone at the end of the month.

But now suppose you send that same worker off to a training seminar for a week. His salary and the seminar fee have been spent on something that is not "gone" at the end of the month. Whatever he has learned persists in his head through the coming months. If you've spent your training money wisely, it is an investment, perhaps a very good one. But, by accounting convention, we expense it anyway.

So Who Cares?

What matters is not so much how the bean counters must report these things to the IRS or to the stockholders, but how managers think about the amount their company has invested in its people. This human capital can be substantial; thinking about it erroneously as sunk expense may lead managers toward actions that fail to preserve the value of an organization's investment.

Of course, "actions that fail to preserve the value of an organization's investment" are a staple of imperfect management. Companies go through periods in which middle and upper managers vie to outdo each other in thinking up ways to improve near-term performance (quarterly earnings) by sacrificing the longer term. This is usually called "bottom-line consciousness," but we prefer to give it another name: "eating the seed corn."

Assessing the Investment in Human Capital

How much does your company have invested in you and your colleagues? An easy way to get a handle on this amount is to consider what happens when one of you leaves: Suppose, for example, that Louise, your database expert, announces she will depart at the end of the month. Prior to this, you had been feeling pretty good about prospects that your five-person team would be able to deliver a new version of your company's sales-capture system by next summer. The tasks had been moving along smoothly, and the team was well-knit and highly effective. At least it was before Louise dropped her bombshell. Now, who knows? What a disaster. You get Personnel on the phone and give the bad news. "Louise is leaving on the thirty-first," you report. Then you ask, hopefully, "Can you get me another Louise?"

Unfortunately, Personnel is fresh out of experts with Louise's grasp of the requirements, the technology, the domain, and the people involved. "How about a Ralph?" your contact suggests. You have never heard of Ralph, nor has anyone else on the team, but he seems to be the only game in town, so you agree. The deal is done. Louise leaves on the thirty-first, and Ralph moves in the next day.

In one sense, the project has experienced no disruption at all. You had five people on the thirty-first, and you've got five people again on the first. If Ralph earns about the same as Louise, the company is dutifully buying people-time for you at the same rate as last month, and the team will be supplied with precisely five person-months this month, exactly as it would have been if Louise had stayed on. If the project was on-schedule last month, it should still be on-schedule now. So what are you bellyaching about?

Well, let's look at how Ralph spends his first day with the company. There was a certain amount of database work remaining that Louise left on her plate when she departed; how much does Ralph chip away of that remaining work on Day One? Of course, the answer is, *nothing.* He doesn't do squat. He spends the whole day filling out forms for his health insurance, learning how to order-in lunch, getting his supplies, configuring his workstation, and having his PC connected to the network. His net production is zero. Whoops, it may even be less than zero. If he uses up any of the other people's time—and you know he is going to, just to get his basic questions answered—then his net contribution to team production for the day will be negative.

Okay, that's Day One; how about Day Two? Day Two is a little better. Ralph is now fully involved, reading the notes that Louise left for him. This is work that Louise wouldn't have had to do herself had she stayed on, since she knew all that stuff cold. (She wouldn't have had to write the notes either if she hadn't been about to leave.) Ralph's production rate is still far lower than Louise's would have been. He may still have a negative effect, since he is still likely to need help from the rest of the team, using up time that team members would have applied to the work had they not had Ralph to support.

Eventually, your new teammate is completely up to speed, producing at more or less the same rate that Louise did. Real productivity of the database worker position over time looks something like Figure 20–3.

Productivity took a hit when Louise left, even passing below zero for a while as others scurried to make up for the loss of a well-integrated team member. Then, eventually, it worked its way up to where it was before.

The shaded area on the graph represents the lost production (work that didn't get done) caused by Louise's departure. Or, viewed differently, it is the investment that the company is now making to get Ralph up where Louise was after the company's past investments in her skills and capabilities.

Figure 20–3   Lost production due to change of personnel.

We could put a dollar figure on the shaded area based on how much the organization had to pay for time that wasn't productive. If it takes Ralph six months to get up to speed and his progress is essentially linear, then the investment is approximately half the total time—that is, three person-months of effort. The dollar figure for this investment is whatever the company pays Ralph for salary and overhead during three months.

What Is the Ramp-Up Time for an Experienced Worker?

Six months to progress from being a slightly negative producer to performing at the rate of your predecessor? This might be a reasonable provision for a new applications programmer, but it probably wouldn't be nearly enough for anyone joining a team that does even slightly more sophisticated work. When we oblige our clients to put a figure on ramp-up time for new workers, most have to allow far longer than six months. One of our clients, a builder of network protocol analyzers and packet sniffers, estimates that it takes more than two years to bring a new worker up to speed. The client only hires people who have a firm grasp of the underlying technology, so the two years is the added time to learn the specific domain and to fit into the team. The net capital investment in each new worker is therefore something like $200,000.

Now suppose there is another round of lean-and-mean downsizing, and the company has to consider laying off such a person. Yes, the ongoing expense of the worker's salary and overhead would be saved, but the $200,000 investment would be lost. If the company takes account of this fact, it might see that it can't possibly afford to lay off such a valuable resource.

Playing Up to Wall Street

Through years of layoffs, cutbacks, downsizings, right-sizings, and retractions, Wall Street has applauded each and every cut as though such retreat were the object of the exercise. It's worth pointing out that it isn't:

The object of the exercise is upsizing, not downsizing.

Companies that downsize are frankly admitting that their upper management has blown it.

But Wall Street still applauds. Why is that? Part of the reason is that it looks so good on the books. A few thousand employees gone, and every penny they would have earned goes right to the bottom line, or at least it seems to. What's conveniently forgotten in this analysis is the investment in those people—paid for with real, hard-earned dollars and now thrown out the window as if it had no value.

There is probably no hope of changing the view that Wall Street takes of treating investment in people as an expense. But companies that play this game will suffer in the long run. The converse is also true: Companies that manage their investment sensibly will prosper in the long run. Companies of knowledge workers have to realize that it is their investment in human capital that matters most. The good ones already do.

PART IV

Growing Productive Teams

Think back over a particularly enjoyable work experience from your career. What was it that made the experience such a pleasure? The simplistic answer is, "Challenge." Good work experiences have always got a fair measure of challenge about them.

Now think of a specific enjoyable memory from that period. Play it over in your mind like a video. Maybe it was a meeting or a bull session or an all-nighter or the breakfast that followed one. If you're like most of us, such memories are vivid and surprisingly complete. You can hear the sounds and individual voices, you can see expressions on faces, you're aware of the setting. Freeze your mental video now and examine a single frame in detail. Where is the challenge? We're willing to bet that it doesn't figure into your memory at all, or if it does, it's a remote part of the background.

What's in the foreground of most of our prized work memories is team interaction. When a group of people fuse into a meaningful whole, the entire character of the work changes. The challenge of the work is important, but not in and of itself; it is important because it gives us something to focus on *together*. The challenge is the instrument for our coming together. In the best work groups, the ones in which people have the most fun and perform at their upper limits, team interactions are everything. They are the reason that people stick it out, put their all into the work, overcome enormous obstacles.

People work better and have more fun when the team comes together. Part IV looks into the concept of the successfully bonded team and things you can do to help such teams happen.

21

The Whole Is Greater Than the Sum of the Parts

We tend to use the word *team* fairly loosely in the business world, calling any group of people assigned to work together a "team." But many of these groups just don't seem like teams. They don't have a common definition of success or any identifiable team spirit. Something is missing. What is missing is a phenomenon we call *jell*.

Concept of the Jelled Team

A jelled team is a group of people so strongly knit that the whole is greater than the sum of the parts. The production of such a team is greater than that of the same people working in unjelled form. Just as important, the enjoyment that people derive from their work is greater than what you'd expect given the nature of the work itself. In some cases, jelled teams working on assignments that others would declare downright dull have a simply marvelous time.

Once a team begins to jell, the probability of success goes up dramatically. The team can become almost unstoppable, a juggernaut for success. Managing these juggernaut teams is a real pleasure. You spend most of your time just getting obstacles out of their way, clearing the path so that bystanders don't get trampled underfoot: "Here they come, folks. Stand back and hold onto your hats." They don't need to be managed in the traditional sense, and they certainly don't need to be motivated. They've got *momentum.*

The reasons for this effect are not so complex: Teams by their very nature are formed around goals. (Think of the sports team: Could it even exist without a goal?) Prior to a team's jelling, the individuals on the team might have had a diversity of goals. But as part of the jelling process, they have all bought into the common goal. This corporate goal takes on an enhanced importance because of its significance to the group. Even though the goal itself may seem arbitrary to team members, they pursue it with enormous energy.

Management by Hysterical Optimism

Some managers are disturbed by the sentiments of the preceding paragraph. They find it distasteful to consider any artifice for getting workers to accept corporate goals. Why should we need to form elaborate social units to do that? After all, professional workers are supposed to accept their employer's goals as a condition of employment. That's what it means to be a professional.

Believing that workers will automatically accept organizational goals is the sign of naïve managerial optimism. The mechanism by which individuals involve themselves in the organization's objectives is more complex than that. You wouldn't be surprised to learn, for example, that the fellow you know as a database specialist is more inclined to describe himself as a father, a Boy Scout leader, and a member of the local school board. In these roles, he makes thoughtful value judgments all the time. What would be a surprise is if he stopped making value judgments when he arrived at work. He doesn't. He is continually at work examining each claim for his individual energies and loyalty. Organizational goals come in for constant scrutiny by the people who work for the organization, and most of those goals are judged to be awfully arbitrary.

The dilemma here is that as boss, you have probably accepted the corporate goal (bring the project home by next April for less than $750,000), and accepted it wholeheartedly. If your staff isn't just as enthusiastic, you're disappointed. Their lack of interest might seem almost treasonous to you. But hold on here: Is it possible that *your own* strong identification with a corporate goal stems from something beyond mere professionalism? Isn't it true that some artful engineering on the part of your boss and the powers above has made that corporate goal line up exactly with one of your own? Meeting the corporate aims is certain to lead directly to more authority and responsibility for you: "Today the Sysboombah Project, tomorrow the world!" Throughout the upper ranks of the organization, there is marvelous ingenuity at work to be sure that each manager has a strong personal incentive to accept the corporate goals. Only at the bottom, where the real work is performed, does this ingenuity fail. There we count on "professionalism" and nothing else to assure that people are all pulling in the same direction. Lots of luck.

If you work for the Save the Snaildarters Foundation or the First Fiberoni Church of Holy Purity or any other organization in which all employees are bound together by common belief, then you may be able to count on their natural affinity for the organization's goals. Otherwise, forget it. While the executive committee may get itself all heated up over a big increase in profits, this same objective is pretty small potatoes to people at the bottom of the heap. PROFIT UP ONE BILLION DOLLARS AT MEGALITHIC INC. Ho-hum. COMPANY LOGS RECORD QUARTER. Zzzzzzzz.

I once ran a telecommunications project for a large consumer finance company. This organization was in the business of lending money to poor people at outlandishly high rates of interest, a business that back then was illegal in 23 states. Increasing the company's already huge profit was not something the average worker could easily identify with, but management seemed to think it was. A delegation came to talk to me late one Friday afternoon. The company's chances for the best second quarter in history were in our hands, they said. They asked me to share this fact with the rest of the team, "to focus their efforts." I had never worked on a more focused team in my life, but I dutifully passed the word on the next morning. (They were so fired up that the whole team was in, even though it was a Saturday.) The energy went out of the team like wind out of a sail. The chief programmer summed it all up: "Who gives a rat's ass for their second quarter?" Half an hour later, they'd all gone home.

—TDM

Getting the system built was an arbitrary goal, but the team had accepted it. It was what they had formed around. From the time of jelling, the team itself had been the real focus for their energies. They were in it for joint success, the pleasure of achieving the goal, any goal, together. Refocusing their attention on the company's interest in the project didn't help. It just made success seem trivial and meaningless.

The Guns of Navarone

Goals of corporations are always going to seem arbitrary to people—corporations seem arbitrary to people—but the arbitrariness of goals doesn't mean no one is ever going to accept them. If it did, we wouldn't have sports. The goals in sports are always utterly arbitrary. The Universe doesn't care whether the little white ball goes between the posts at Argentina's end of the field or those at Italy's. But a lot of people get themselves very involved in the outcome. Their involvement is a function of the social units they belong to.

Those at the periphery of a team may be mildly interested in the team's success or failure, but their interest is tiny compared to that of the team members. People who work on jelled teams often get so involved that they're psyched up enough to storm the guns of Navarone, all just to pass the version 3 acceptance test for the pension trust system. You have to remind them that what they're striving to accomplish is not the Moral Equivalent of War.

In spite of the useful energy and enthusiasm that characterize jelled teams, managers don't take particular pains to foster them. Part of the reason is an imperfect understanding of why teams matter. The manager who is strongly motivated toward goal attainment is likely to observe that teams don't attain goals; people on the teams attain goals. Virtually all of the component tasks required to meet the objective are performed by the individuals who make up the team. Most of this work is done by individuals working alone.

There is very little true teamwork required in most of our work. But teams are still important, for they serve as a device to get everyone pulling in the same direction.

The purpose of a team is not goal attainment but goal alignment.

When the team is fulfilling its purpose, team members are more effective because they're more directed.

Signs of a Jelled Team

A few very characteristic signs indicate that a jelled team has occurred. The most important of these is *low turnover* during projects and in the middle of well-defined tasks. The team members aren't going anywhere till the work is done. Things that matter enormously prior to jell (money, status, position for advancement) matter less or not at all after jell. People certainly aren't about to leave their team for a rinky-dink consideration like a little more salary. Sadly, managers often miss this strong indication of their own success. They are disinclined to pay attention to turnover even when it's killing them; when turnover is low, they don't think about it at all.

Jelled teams are usually marked by a *strong sense of identity*. The teams you hear discussed in the industry have colorful names: the "Okie Coders" at General Electric, or the "Gang of Four" at DuPont, or the "Chaos Group" at Cincinnati Gas & Electric. Teammates may all use the same catch phrases and share many in-jokes. There may be obvious team space. The teams may congregate at lunch or hang out at the same watering hole after work.

There is a *sense of eliteness* on a good team. Team members feel they're part of something unique. They feel they're better than the run of the mill.

They have a cocky, SWAT Team attitude that may be faintly annoying to people who aren't part of the group.

There is invariably a feeling of *joint ownership of the product* built by the jelled team. Participants are pleased to have their names grouped together on a product or a part of one. The individual is eager for peer review. The team space is decorated with views of the product as it approaches completion.

The final sign of a jelled team is the *obvious enjoyment* that people take in their work. Jelled teams just feel healthy. The interactions are easy and confident and warm.

Teams and Cliques

If it made you at all uneasy to read about jelled teams sticking to themselves and feeling slightly superior to the rest of the world, you're not the only one. We can almost hear you thinking, "Wait a minute, what these guys are calling a 'team' may be what we would call a 'clique.' Teams may be good, but aren't cliques something to be avoided at all cost?"

The difference between a team and a clique is like the difference between a breeze and a draft. *Breeze* and *draft* have identical meanings: They both mean "cool current of air." If you find that cool current of air delightful, you call it a breeze; if you find it annoying, you call it a draft. The connotations are different, but the denotation is the same. Similarly, there is no difference in denotation between a team and a clique, but the connotations are opposite. People use *team* when the tight bonding of the jelled working group is pleasing to them. And they use *clique* when it represents a threat.

Fear of cliques is a sign of managerial insecurity. The greater the insecurity, the more frightening the idea of a clique can be. There are reasons for this: Managers are often not true members of their teams (more about this in Chapter 28, "Chemistry for Team Formation"), so the loyalties that exclude them are stronger than the ones that bind them into the group. The loyalties within the group are stronger than those tying the group to the company. Then there is the awful thought that a tightly knit team may leave en masse and take all of its energy and enthusiasm over to the competition. For all these reasons, the insecure manager is threatened by cliques. He or she would feel better working with a staff of uniform plastic people, identical, interchangeable, and unbonded.

The jelled work group may be cocky and self-sufficient, irritating and exclusive, but it does more to serve the manager's real goals than any assemblage of interchangeable parts could ever do.

22
The Black Team

The value of jelled teams will be obvious to you if you have already had the enjoyable experience of working on one. But just in case you haven't, this chapter is intended to give you some sense of what they're like. Presented below is the story of a legendary team that began to make its mark in the 1960s. Some of the lore of this team must surely be exaggerated, but it makes a good yarn, and at least most of it is true.

The Stuff of Which Legends Are Made

Back in the dawn of time (relatively speaking), there was a company in upper New York State that made large blue computers. The company also made software to run on these computers. Customers of this company were nice enough folks, but just between us, they could be awfully poor sports about software delivered with bugs. For a while, the company put its efforts into training the customers to make them more tolerant of bugs. But this approach didn't work out, so they bit the bullet and decided to get rid of the bugs instead.

The easy and obvious approach was to have the programmers remove all bugs prior to delivery. For some reason, this didn't work too well either. It seems that the programmers (at least the ones back in those days) were rather too inclined to believe the best of their programs. Try as they might, they couldn't find the last remaining bugs, so they often declared the software to be done when there were still lots of bugs.

Finding the last bug was hard, but some testers were better than others. The company formed a group of these particularly talented testers and gave them the charter to do final testing on critical software before it was sent to the customers. Thus was born the legendary Black Team.

The Black Team was initially made up of people who had proved themselves to be slightly better at testing than their peers. They were slightly more motivated. They also were testing code that had been written by someone else, so they were free of the cognitive dissonance that hampers developers when testing their own programs. All in all, those who formed the team might have expected it to achieve at least a modest improvement in product quality, but they didn't expect more than that. What they got was much more than that.

The most surprising thing about the Black Team was not how good it was at the beginning, but how much it improved during the next year. Some magic was happening: The team was forming a personality of its own. This personality was being shaped by an adversary philosophy of testing that evolved among group members, a philosophy that they had to want and expect to find defects. They weren't rooting for the developers at all, quite the opposite. They were delighting in submitting the program (and the programmer) to a sequence that was not just a test, but an ordeal. Bringing your program in for Black Team testing was like appearing before Ming the Merciless.

Pitiful Earthlings, What Can Save You Now?

At first it was simply a joke that the tests they ran were mean and nasty, and that the team members actually loved to make your code fail. Then it wasn't a joke at all. They began to cultivate an image of destroyers. What they destroyed was not only your code but your whole day. They did monstrously unfair things to elicit failure, overloading the buffers, comparing empty files, and keying in outrageous input sequences. Grown men and women were reduced to tears by watching their programs misbehave under the demented handling of these fiends. The worse they made you feel, the more they enjoyed it.

To enhance the growing image of nastiness, team members began to dress in black (hence the name Black Team). They took to cackling horribly whenever a program failed. Some of the members grew long mustaches that they could twirl in Simon Legree fashion. They'd get together and work out ever-more-awful testing ploys. Programmers began to mutter about the diseased minds on the Black Team.

Needless to say, the company was delighted. Every defect the team found was one that the customers wouldn't find. The team was a success. It succeeded as a test group, but more important for our purposes here, it succeeded as a social unit. People on the team got such a kick out of what they were doing that colleagues outside the team were positively jealous. The black out-fits and the silly exaggerated behavior were part of the fun, but there was something much more fundamental going on. The chemistry within the group had become an end in itself.

Footnote

Over time, members of the team moved on one at a time to other things. Since the team function was important to the company, departing members were replaced immediately. This continued until finally there wasn't a single member left of the original group. But there was still a Black Team. The team survived the loss of all of its original staff, and it emerged with its energy and its personality intact.

23

Teamicide

What's called for here is a concise chapter entitled "Making Teams Jell at Your Company." It should have half a dozen simple prescriptions for good team formation. These prescriptions should be enough to guarantee jelled teams. In the planning stage of this work, that is exactly the chapter we expected to write. We were confident. How difficult could it be to cut to the heart of the matter and give the reader practical tools to aid the process of making teams jell? We would apply all our skills, all our experience; we would overwhelm the problem with logic and pure brilliance. That's how it looked in the planning stage. . . .

Between plan and execution, there were a few distressing encounters with reality. The first of these was that we just couldn't come up with the six prescriptions needed for the chapter. We got stuck at zero. We'd been prepared to scale our expectations down a bit, but not this much. ("Zero Things You Can Do to Make Teams Jell"?) It seemed clear that something was wrong with the underlying notion of the chapter. What was wrong was the whole idea of making teams jell. You can't make teams jell. You can hope they will jell; you can cross your fingers; you can act to improve the odds of jelling—but you can't make it happen. The process is much too fragile to be controlled.

Part of our scaling down of expectations involved a change in vocabulary. We stopped talking about *building* teams, and talked instead of *growing* them. The agricultural image seemed right. Agriculture isn't entirely controllable. You enrich the soil, you plant seeds, you water according to the latest theory, and you hold your breath. You just might get a crop; you might not. If it all comes up roses, you'll feel fine, but next year you'll be sweating it out again. That's pretty close to how team formation works.

Back to brainstorming mode: We began looking for "Six Things You Can Do to Make Team Formation Possible." It was still hard. At last, in desperation, we tried a trick called *inversion,* described in Edward deBono's *Lateral Thinking.* When you're stuck trying to solve a problem, deBono suggests that rather than looking for ways to achieve your goal, look for ways to achieve the exact opposite of your goal. This can have the effect of clearing away the brain's cobwebs that keep you from being creative. So instead of looking for ways to make team formation possible, we began to think of ways to make it impossible. That was easy. In no time at all, we came up with lots of surefire ways to inhibit the formation of teams and disrupt project sociology. These measures, taken together, constitute a strategy we dubbed *teamicide.* Our short list of teamicide techniques is

- Defensive management
- Bureaucracy
- Physical separation
- Fragmentation of people's time
- Quality reduction of the product
- Phony deadlines
- Clique control

Some of these techniques will look awfully familiar. They are things that companies do all the time.

Defensive Management

It makes good sense for you, the manager, to take a defensive posture in most areas of risk. If you must work with a piece of failure-prone gear, you get a backup; if the client is inclined to vacillate, you take pains to nail down the product specifications; if a contract vendor tends to "forget" promises, you publish minutes after each meeting.

There's one area, though, where defensiveness will always backfire: You can't protect yourself against your own people's incompetence. If your staff isn't up to the job at hand, you will fail. Of course, if the people are badly suited to the job, you should get new people. But once you've decided to go with a given group, your best tactic is to trust them. Any defensive measure taken to guarantee success in spite of them will only make things worse. It may give you some relief from worry in the short term, but it won't help in the long run, and it will poison any chance for the team to jell.

I found myself one day giving Consultant's Speech Number 9B to a project group, chastising them because they'd failed to get client approval for their emerging concept of a new system. They all looked faintly embarrassed. Finally, one of them said, "We all agree that the client ought to be seeing this stuff. But our boss has laid down a firm rule that nothing will ever be shown to people outside the project unless it has his approval." She went on to explain that the boss was so swamped that months of work had piled up in his In-box. What option did they have? They were just plugging away in the dark knowing full well that most of what they were producing wouldn't pass muster with the client staff when it was finally shown to them.

—TRL

The boss didn't trust his own people. He was worried they might show something that was wrong to client personnel. He was worried that their errors might reflect badly on him. Only his own judgment was competent; anyone else's was suspect.

If you're the manager, of course you're going to feel that your judgment is better than that of people under you. You have more experience and perhaps a higher standard of excellence than they have; that's how you got to be the manager. At any point in the project where you don't interpose your own judgment, your people are more likely to make a mistake. So what? Let them make some mistakes. That doesn't mean you can't override a decision (very occasionally) or give specific direction to the project. But if the staff comes to believe it's not allowed to make any errors of its own, the message that you don't trust them comes through loud and clear. There is no message you can send that will better inhibit team formation.

Most managers give themselves excellent grades on knowing when to trust their people and when not to. But in our experience, too many managers err on the side of mistrust. They follow the basic premise that their people may operate completely autonomously, as long as they operate correctly. This amounts to no autonomy at all. The only freedom that has any meaning is the freedom to proceed differently from the way your manager would have proceeded. This is true in a broader sense, too: The right to be right (in your manager's eyes or in your government's eyes) is irrelevant; it's only the right to be wrong that makes you free.

The most obvious defensive management ploys are prescriptive Methodologies ("My people are too dumb to build systems without them.") and technical interference by the manager. Both are doomed to fail in the long run. In addition, they make for efficient teamicide. People who feel untrusted have little inclination to bond together into a cooperative team.

Bureaucracy

Studies conducted by Capers Jones in the 1970s and 1980s reported on systems development costs by work category. One of the categories was "Paperwork." What Jones calls *paperwork* is more or less mindless paper pushing, since the thinking time necessary to decide what to put on the paper is categorized as some other activity, such as analysis, design, or test planning. In other words, his "paperwork" category is pure bureaucracy. Jones concluded that paperwork is the second largest category of systems development work. It accounts for more than 30 percent of the cost of producing a given product.

There is a depressing modern trend to make development workers more and more into bureaucrats. Perhaps this is a sign of epidemic defensive management. But while the trend is global, it is not at all uniform. We know of companies in which the development groups look and feel like a bureaucratic nightmare by Kafka, and other companies in which the paperwork burden is minuscule.

Mindless paper pushing is a waste. It ought to be attacked because it keeps people from working. But our point here is a slightly different one. It is that bureaucracy hurts team formation. The team needs to believe in whatever goal it forms around. That goal can be arbitrary, but at least it has to exist. There has to be some evidence that management believes in it. Just telling your people that the goal matters won't be enough if you also have to tell them they should spend a third of their time pushing paper. Paper pushers just can't get themselves into SWAT Team mode. They can't see themselves hell-bent for success.

Physical Separation

When the Furniture Police makes its case for the Zippo-Flippo Modular Office System, all the talk is of "flexibility." But when it comes time to flex a bit to put a work group together, the long faces come out. "We can't disrupt everything and move stuff around over our lovely carpet just to get these four people into adjacent space. Can't they text?" The result is that what could be a tightly bound team is scattered over multiple floors or even in different buildings. The specific work interactions may not suffer terribly, but there is no casual interaction. Group members may grow stronger bonds to nongroup neighbors, just because they see more of them. There is no group space, no immediate and constant reinforcement, no chance of a group culture forming. (You couldn't imagine Black Team members all dressing in black if their work spaces were not together; they'd be constantly interacting with people who weren't in on the joke, who just thought they were bizarre, and the whole funny bit would die with a whimper.)

Physical separation of people who are expected to interact closely doesn't make much sense anyway. Neighboring workers are a source of noise and disruption. When they're all on the same team, they tend to go into quiet mode at the same time, so there is less interruption of flow. Putting them together also gives them opportunity for the casual interaction that is so necessary for team formation.

Fragmentation of Time

One of my clients is an agency of the Australian government. During one consulting call, I collected data indicating that the average worker there was involved in four or more different projects. I complained about this to the Commissioner. He said it was regrettable, but just a fact of life. People's duties were fragmented because their skills and knowledge made them indispensable to efforts other than the principal ones they were assigned to. He said it was inevitable. I said it was nonsense. I proposed that he make it a specific policy that people be assigned to one and only one project at a time and that the policy be written down and widely distributed. He was game. A year later, when I returned, the average worker was assigned to fewer than two projects.

—TDM

Fragmentation is bad for team formation, but it's also bad for efficiency. (Perhaps you've begun to pick up a trend here.) People can keep track of only so many human interactions. When they try to be part of four working groups, they have four times as many interactions to track. They spend all their time changing gears.

No one can be part of multiple jelled teams. The tight interactions of the jelled team are exclusive. Enough fragmentation and teams just won't jell. The saddest thing is we allow far more fragmentation than is really necessary. We tend to concede this battle without even a fight. Simply saying that a goal is to assign people only one piece of work at a time can result in significant reductions of fragmentation, and thus give teams a real chance to form.

The Quality-Reduced Product

The heading used here is a facetious one; nobody really talks about quality-reduced products. What they talk about is cost-reduced products. But it usually boils down to the same thing. The typical steps we take to deliver a product in less time result in lower quality. Often the product's end user gives willing consent to this trade-off (less quality for earlier, cheaper delivery). But such concessions can be very painful for the developers. Their self-esteem and enjoyment are undermined by the necessity of building a product of clearly lower quality than what they are capable of.

An early casualty of quality reduction is whatever sense of team identification the group has been able to build. Co-workers who are developing a shoddy product don't even want to look each other in the eye. There is no joint sense of accomplishment in store for them. They know that there will be a general sense of relief when they can stop doing what they're doing. At the end of the project, they'll make every effort to separate themselves from other members of the group, and get on to better things.

Phony Deadlines

In Chapter 3, "Vienna Waits for You," we made the point that tight deadlines can sometimes be demotivating. But there are certainly cases where a tight but not impossible deadline can constitute an enjoyable challenge to the team. What's never going to help, however, is a *phony* deadline. When the manager intones, "We absolutely must be done by _____," group members can barely keep their eyes from rolling. They've been there before. They know the whole routine.

Maybe phony deadlines used to work. Maybe there were once workers so naïve that they actually believed what they heard. When the boss said the job "absolutely, *positively* has to be done by January," maybe they just accepted it and buckled down. Maybe. But it certainly doesn't work that way anymore. The people on your staff will know if they're being bamboozled. If you say the product absolutely has to be out the door by some arbitrary date, they will ask, "Why? Will the universe grind to a halt if we're late? Will the company fold? Will the nation slide into the sea? Will Western Civilization break down?"

In the typical phony deadline spiel, the manager announces that the work must be done on such and such a date. The date mentioned is impossible to meet, and everyone knows it. The effort will certainly slip (so much for the idea that the deadline is absolute). The work has been defined in such a way that success is impossible. The message to the workers is clear: The boss is a Parkinsonian robot with no respect or concern for them. The boss believes they won't do a stroke of work except under duress. Don't expect a jelled team on that project.

Clique Control

A participant at one of our seminars made this observation: "The only time our management shows any awareness of teams is when it takes specific steps to break them up." There may be an explicit policy that teams can't be allowed to stay together from one job to another. Or, there may be a policy that projects winding down have to be de-staffed smoothly over time so that the personnel organization can steer people efficiently into new projects. This assures that teams will be broken up. Still other organizations take no specific steps to disband teams, but miss every opportunity to keep them together.

The pleasures of team activity and the energy that is produced by team interaction are articles of faith in our society. How did business organizations ever come to be so apathetic or even antipathetic toward teams? Part of the reason is insecurity, as indicated in Chapter 22, "The Black Team." Another part is a conspicuously low consciousness of teams in upper management. The team phenomenon, as we've described it, is something that happens only at the bottom of the hierarchy. For all the talk about "management teams," there really is no such thing—certainly never jelled teams at the managerial level. When managers are bonded into teams, it's only because they serve dual roles: manager on the one hand and group member on the other. They become accepted as part-time peers by the people they manage. As you go higher and higher in the organization chart, the concept of jelled teams recedes further and further into oblivion.

Once More Over the Same Depressing Ground

Most organizations don't set out consciously to kill teams. They just act that way.

24

Teamicide Revisited

T he seven kinds of teamicide we described in the previous chapter seemed to us (when we wrote the first edition) to stretch all the way from the alpha to the omega of the subject. But there were two important kinds of teamicide that we missed. Like the original seven, these two are practiced widely in our field. One of them has become so ubiquitous that a small growth industry has sprung up to support it. . . .

Those Damn Posters and Plaques

Pick up the airline magazine or on-board shoppers' catalog on your next flight and flip through the full-page advertisements. Somewhere in there you will come upon a colorful selection of inspirational posters and framed messages for display on corporate walls (lest someone use up the wall space with work products). Don't just glance at them, but force yourself to read through them all, turning over their texts in your mind and savoring their syrupy prose. If you're not angry by the time you're done, you may have been serving under lousy managers for much too much of your career.

Most forms of teamicide do their damage by effectively demeaning the work, or demeaning the people who do it. Teams are catalyzed by a common sense that the work is important and that doing it well is worthwhile. The word *well* in this last sentence is essential: The team assigns itself the task of setting and upholding a standard of prideful workmanship. All team members understand that the quality of the work is important to the organization, but the team adopts a still higher standard to distinguish itself. Without this distinguishing factor, the group is just a group, never a real team.

151

Into this complicated mix, now imagine dropping a $150 framed poster to advise people that "Quality Is Job One." Oh. Gee, we never would have thought that. No sir, we sort of assumed—until this wonderful poster came along—that Quality was Job Twenty-nine, or maybe Eleventy-seven, or maybe even lower than that on the corporate value scale, maybe someplace after reducing ear wax or sorting the trash. But now we know. Thanks.

These *motivational accessories,* as they are called (including slogan coffee mugs, plaques, pins, key chains, and awards), are a triumph of form over substance. They seem to extol the importance of Quality, Leadership, Creativity, Teamwork, Loyalty, and a host of other organizational virtues. But they do so in such simplistic terms as to send an entirely different message: Management here believes that these virtues can be improved with posters rather than by hard work and managerial talent. Everyone quickly understands that the presence of the posters is a sure sign of the absence of hard work and talent.

That important matters like these should be the subject of motivational posters is already an insult. But the implementation makes it even worse. Consider an example marketed by one company: It shows a soft-focus image of sweating oarsmen, rowing in perfect unison through the misty morning. Underneath it reads, in part,

T•E•A•M•W•O•R•K
The Fuel That Allows Common People To Attain
Uncommon Results

The "common people" they're talking about here are you and your workmates. Common people. (Don't take it too hard.) At least they're consistent in attitude: The same company's Leadership poster tells us that "the speed of the leader determines the rate of the pack." The pack. Yep, that's you again.

Motivational accessories are phony enough to make most people's skin crawl. They do harm in healthy organizations. The only place where they do no harm is where they are ignored—as in companies where the harm was done long, long ago and people have ceased to register any further decline.

Overtime: An Unanticipated Side Effect

You may already have picked up a certain bias in this book's original chapters against the use of overtime. It has been our experience that the positive potential of working extra hours is far exaggerated, and that its negative impact is almost never considered. That negative impact can be substantial: error, burnout, accelerated turnover, and compensatory undertime. In this section, we examine yet another negative effect of overtime: its teamicidal repercussions on otherwise healthy work groups.

Imagine a project with a well-jelled team. You and your colleagues are producing good work at a rate that is frankly astonishing, even to you and your boss. You all understand this to be the beneficial effect of team jell, that the whole of your team production capacity is greater than the sum of your individual productivities. But it's still not enough. The powers that be have promised the product for June, and it's just not going to get done at the current rate.

Sounds like a case for a little overtime, right? You move the team into high gear, add a few hours to the workweek (still at the same high production rate), maybe work a few Saturdays. There is only one problem: One of your teammates—let's call him Allen—just doesn't have the flexibility that the rest of you enjoy. He is a widower and thus the primary caregiver for his little boy. Allen has to show up at the day-care facility at 5:15 each afternoon to pick the child up. As you might imagine, his Saturdays and Sundays, the only real quality time with his son, are inviolable.

"Hey, that's okay," you think. "We'll cover for Allen. We all understand." And you all do . . . in the beginning.

A few months later, however, the rest of you are starting to show the strain. All your Saturdays have been gobbled up, as have most of your Sundays. You've been working sixty-plus hours a week for longer than you thought possible, and your spouses and kids are grumbling. Your laundry is piling up, your bills are unpaid, your vacation plans have been scrapped. Allen, through all this, is still working a forty-hour week. Finally, somebody says what you are all thinking: "I'm getting pretty sick of carrying Allen."

What's happened here? A team that was positively humming with the good effects of jell has been pried apart by an overtime policy that could not be applied uniformly to the team members. But the members of good teams are never uniform in any respect, certainly not in their abilities to "borrow" time from their personal lives. In almost any team of four or five or six people, there are bound to be a few who can't be expected to put in the kind of overtime that might fit pretty well into some of the others' lives. All that can be shrugged off as unimportant if the overtime is only a matter of a few long evenings and maybe one extra weekend day. But if the overtime drags on over months and starts to exact a real toll on even the most willing team members, there is bound to be damage to team cohesion. The people who aren't sharing the pain will become, little by little, estranged from the others. And the team magic will be gone.

Extended overtime is a productivity-reduction technique, anyway. The extra hours are almost always more than offset by the negative side effects. This is true even if you don't consider the disruption of the team. When you take into account the way that the team members' differing abilities to work over-time tends to destroy teams, the case against it becomes persuasive.

Most managers have at least a suspicion that overtime doesn't help, that projects that work a lot of overtime are not much of a credit to their managers' skills and talents. But they end up allowing or encouraging overtime, anyway. Why is this? Consultant and author Jerry Weinberg has an answer of sorts: He suggests that we don't work overtime so much to get the work done on time as to shield ourselves from blame when the work inevitably doesn't get done on time.[1]

---

1. Private communication, Fort Collins, Colorado, 1990.

25
Competition

The issue of competition within a team or work group is a complicated one, something that managers tend to disagree about. You've surely heard the line that companies exist to compete with each other, so by extension, a little competition within the company is a healthy way to keep the competitive edge. Other managers conclude that something is wrong when team members feel they are being pitted against each other. At the extreme, at least, competition is certain to inhibit team jell. If team members are told, for example, that only the best one of them will be around next year, you can be sure that they will not succeed in working together very well.

Consider an Analogy

Like managers, parents sometimes have to grapple with the issue of internal competition. They may find that their children tend to be competitive with each other. They may also try to reassure themselves that the competitive edge will be useful in the rough and tumble of later life, so perhaps honing that competitive edge within the family is okay.

But competition between siblings is not entirely okay. We know, for example, that highly competitive siblings tend to grow up to be distanced from each other, while those who are less competitive as children have at least a chance of building warm sibling friendships as adults. Chances are that you know of at least one example of siblings who "don't speak" as adults, or the saddest extreme, entire families in which no two consecutive siblings have maintained a relationship into adulthood.

There is now a substantial consensus about the ways that parents encourage or discourage sibling competition. Competition is likely to be fostered when children are emotionally undernourished by their parents, when there just isn't enough time, respect, attention, and affection to go around.

Is it possible that internal competition in work teams is fostered by a manager's lack of time, respect, attention, and affection for his or her people? Though that may be too simplistic, we believe there is an important kernel of truth to the idea.

Does It Matter? The Importance of Coaching

What is the long-term effect of heightened competition among people who need to work together? One of the first victims is the easy, effective peer-coaching that is ubiquitous in healthy teams.

As a manager, you may have convinced yourself that you ought to be the principal coach to the team or teams that report to you. That certainly was a common model in the past, when high-tech bosses tended to be proven experts in the technologies their workers needed to master. Today, however, the typical team of knowledge workers has a mix of skills, only some of which the boss has mastered. The boss usually coaches only some of the team members. What of the others? We are increasingly convinced that the team members themselves provide most of the coaching.

When you observe a well-knit team in action, you'll see a basic hygienic act of peer-coaching that is going on all the time. Team members sit down in pairs to transfer knowledge. When this happens, there is always one learner and one teacher. Their roles tend to switch back and forth over time with, perhaps, A coaching B about TCP/IP and then B coaching A about implementation of queues. When it works well, the participants are barely even aware of it. They may not even identify it as coaching; to them, it may just seem like work.

Whether it is named or not, coaching is an important factor in successful team interaction. It provides coordination as well as personal growth to the participants. It also feels good. We tend to look back on significant coaching we've received as a near religious experience. We feel a huge debt to those who have coached us in the past, a debt that we cheerfully discharge by coaching others.

The act of coaching simply cannot take place if people don't feel safe. In a suitably competitive atmosphere, you would be crazy to let anyone see you sitting down to be coached; it would be a clear indication that you knew less than your coach about some subject matter. You would be similarly crazy to coach someone else, as that person may eventually use your assistance to pass you by.

Teamicide Re-revisited

Internal competition has the direct effect of making coaching difficult or impossible. Since coaching is essential to the workings of a healthy team, anything the manager does to increase competition within a team has to be viewed as teamicidal. Here are some of the managerial actions that tend to produce teamicidal side effects:

- Annual salary or merit reviews

- Management by objectives (MBO)

- Praise of certain workers for extraordinary accomplishment

- Awards, prizes, bonuses tied to performance

- Performance measurement in almost any form

But hold on here, aren't these the very things that managers spend much or even most of their time doing? Sadly, yes. And yet these actions are likely to be teamicidal.

In his 1982 book *Out of the Crisis,* W. Edwards Deming set forth his now widely followed "Fourteen Points." Hidden among them, almost as an afterthought, is point 12B:

> *Remove barriers that rob people in management and in engineering of their right to pride of workmanship. This means [among other things] abolishment of the annual or merit rating and of management by objectives.*[1]

Even people who think of themselves as Deming-ites have trouble with this one. They are left gasping, What the hell are we supposed to do instead?

Deming's point is that MBO and its ilk are managerial cop-outs. By using simplistic extrinsic motivators to goad performance, managers excuse themselves from harder matters such as investment, direct personal motivation, thoughtful team formation, staff retention, and ongoing analysis and redesign of work procedures.

Our point here is somewhat more limited: Any action that rewards team members differentially is likely to foster competition. Managers need to take steps to decrease or counteract this effect.

---

1. W. E. Deming, *Out of the Crisis* (Cambridge, Mass.: MIT Center for Advanced Engineering Study, 1982), p. 24.

Mixing Metaphors

We interrupt this message for . . .

A Startling Confession from the Authors

Throughout this book, we have used and discussed the sports team as a metaphor for a well-jelled technical work group; we are now obliged to emphasize here our growing disenchantment with this metaphor.

Most troubling to us these days is what the sports team metaphor implies about competition. Football teams and soccer teams and baseball teams compete within their leagues, but they also promote a good deal of internal competition. Those players who "ride the pines," for example, must feel just the littlest bit competitive toward the first string. Oh sure, they are rooting for them to win, of course, but perhaps not to look too great in the process.

In high school, I was the shortest member of our varsity basketball team. I still remember the guy who had to foul out before I would be put in. His name was Doug Timmerman. He was the most damnably gifted player; he almost never fouled anybody. I loved him like a brother, but still . . .

—TDM

We have all seen sports teams that succeeded in spite of the failure of one of the individuals. We have also seen individual team members have a great night while their team was losing badly. The success or failure of the individual is thus disconnected from the success or failure of the group as a whole. This is an imperfect situation, one that only exacerbates any incipient tendency toward competition.

By contrast, as an example, a choir or glee club makes an almost perfect linkage between the success or failure of the individual and that of the group. (You'll never have people congratulate you on singing your part perfectly while the choir as a whole sings off-key.)

So, belatedly, we need to tell you that the musical ensemble would have been a happier metaphor for what we are trying to do in well-jelled work groups. We're not the only ones, of course, to use the term "team" to describe such a group.

Whether you call it a "team" or an "ensemble" or a "harmonious work group" is not what matters; what matters is helping all parties understand that the success of the individual is tied irrevocably to the success of the whole.

26

A Spaghetti Dinner

Picture yourself a technical worker who's just been assigned to a new project. You know the manager and most of the other project personnel by name, but that's about it. Your first day on the new project is next Monday. On Wednesday before that Monday, you get a call from your boss-to-be. She's having a get-together, she says, for people on the new project. Is there any chance you could come by her place on Thursday evening for dinner with the rest of the team? You're free and want to meet the new group, so you accept.

When you arrive, the whole group is sitting around the living room drinking beer and telling war stories. You join in and tell a few of your own. The client liaison, who has also been invited, does a bit about his department head. Everybody has another beer. You begin to wonder about food. There is no smell of anything cooking and no sign of anyone working in the kitchen. Finally, your boss-to-be admits that she hasn't had time to make dinner, and suggests that the whole crew walk over to a nearby supermarket and assemble the makings of a meal. "I guess we must be capable of putting a spaghetti dinner together."

Team Effects Beginning to Happen

Off you go. In the supermarket, you amble as a group through the aisles. Nobody takes charge. Your boss seems to have anything on her mind but dinner. She chats and laughs and offers up a story about the IRS. In spite of a general lack of direction, some things do get thrown into the cart. One fellow has already gotten the salad pretty well taken care of. There is some talk of making a clam sauce, and when nobody's opposed, two of your new mates begin to talk out the details. You decide to make your patented garlic bread. Someone else picks out a bottle of Chianti. Finally, there is a consensus that enough stuff is in the cart for dinner.

Back at the ranch, you all set down your bags of groceries and the boss grabs another beer and tells about a new software tool. Little by little, the party gravitates toward the kitchen where some preparations are beginning. Your boss gives no direction, but she pitches in to chop onions when someone suggests that's what's needed. You start the garlic and olive oil simmering in a pan. There is a sauce bubbling and some spaghetti boiling. Gradually, a dinner comes together. You all eat till you're full and then share in the cleanup chores.

What's Been Going On Here?

So far, nobody has billed a single day of effort to the project, but you've just had your first success as a group. Success breeds success, and productive harmony breeds more productive harmony. Your chances of jelling into a meaningful team are enhanced by your very first experience together.

Presented this way, the spaghetti dinner may seem like a contrivance on the manager's part. But it probably wasn't and wouldn't have seemed like it had you been there. If you had asked the manager in question what she had in mind for the evening, she would have probably replied in total sincerity, "Dinner." A natural manager has got a subconscious feel for what's good for the team. This feel may govern decisions throughout the project. The entire experience is organized for small, easy, joint successes. You have to look twice to see the manager's hand in any of this; it just seems to be happening.

Variations on the story of the spaghetti dinner have been told to us in different forms and about different managers for years. The common thread is that good managers provide frequent easy opportunities for the team to succeed together. The opportunities may be tiny pilot subprojects, or demonstrations, or simulations, anything that gets the team quickly into the habit of succeeding together. The best success is the one in which there is no evident management, in which the team works as a genial aggregation of peers. The best boss is the one who can manage this over and over again without the team members knowing they've been "managed." These bosses are viewed by their peers as just lucky. Everything seems to break right for them. They get a fired-up team of people, the project comes together quickly, and everyone stays enthusiastic through the end. These managers never break into a sweat. It looks so easy that no one can believe they are managing at all.

27

Open Kimono

G rowing jelled teams is a fairly chancy matter. Nobody does it consistently. Nobody can make it happen, particularly when it would be most useful. Sometimes the mix is wrong. And sometimes the group is staffed with folks who aren't disposed to become part of a team; they're loners and always will be.

In his book *People and Project Management,* Rob Thomsett analyzes certain of the pathologies that interfere with team formation. It makes fascinating reading. However, few of these pathologies are treatable. About the only remedy is to remove certain members from the project because they hurt the chances of a team to jell. That may sound okay in the abstract, but in any specific case you're likely to find such a remedy plain silly. The very person you'd be inclined to do without for this reason will probably be a star in many other respects. Lots of efforts have to proceed (and succeed) without jelled teams.

Having said all that, we know this indisputable fact: Some managers are pretty good at helping teams to jell. They succeed more often than not. In this chapter, we examine one characteristic of these team-oriented managers.

Calling In Well

> *Chances are you've heard of people calling in sick. You may have called in sick a few times yourself. But have you ever thought of calling in well?*
>
> *It'd go like this: You'd get the boss on the line and say, "Listen, I've been sick ever since I started working here, but today I'm well and I won't be in anymore."*[1]

---

1. T. Robbins, *Even Cowgirls Get the Blues* (New York, Bantam Books, 1977), p. 280.

When people talk about an organization that you'd have to be "sick" to work for, they're not referring to physiological sickness. They mean that working in such a place would require them to disregard certain mental survival rules, rules that protect the well-being of the psychological self. The most important of these rules has to do with self-regard. A job situation that hurts your self-regard is itself "sick."

The person who calls in well is ready for work that enhances self-regard. Assignment to such work is an acknowledgment of certain areas of competence, and it provides autonomy and responsibility in these areas. Managers of well workers are careful to respect that autonomy, once granted. They know that a worker's failure will reflect badly on the boss, but that's just the breaks of the game. They're prepared to suffer the occasional setback, a direct result of failure by one of their people. When it happens, they suspect it will be a failure that they themselves would never have caused, had they been doing the work rather than managing it. But so what? You give your best shot to putting the right person in the position, but once he or she is there, you don't second-guess.

This Open Kimono attitude is the exact opposite of defensive management. You take no steps to defend yourself from the people you've put into positions of trust. And all the people under you are in positions of trust. A person you can't trust with any autonomy is of no use to you.

One of my first bosses was Jerry Wiener, who had run a development team for General Electric on the Dartmouth time-sharing project. He later formed a small high-technology company. At the time I came along, the company was about to enter into a contract that was larger than anything it had ever done before. The entire staff was assembled as our corporate lawyer handed Jerry the contract and told him to read it and sign on the last page. "I don't read contracts," Jerry said, and started to sign. "Oh, wait a minute," said the lawyer, "let me go over it one more time."

—TDM

The lesson here is not that you should sign contracts without reading them (though that may not be a terrible rule in cases where you pay counsel to look out for your interests). If you've got the wrong counsel, you're in deep bananas anyway. Managers who are most proficient at getting the work done are likely to be way out of their depth in evaluating contracts for the work. Reading contracts may be little more than a conceit. Jerry had taken great pains to hire the best counsel he could find. He'd certainly looked over other instances of the man's work. This was not the time to be defensive; it was the time to make it clear to everyone that the boss was assuming and depending on competence around him.

It's heady and a little frightening to know that the boss has put part of his or her reputation into the subordinates' hands. It brings out the best in everyone. The team has something meaningful to form around. They're not just getting a job done. They're making sure that the trust that's been placed in them is rewarded. It is this kind of Open Kimono management that gives teams their best chance to form.

The Getaway Ploy

The most common means by which bosses defend themselves from their own people is direct physical oversight. They wander through the work areas, looking for people goofing off or for incompetence about to happen. They are the Parkinsonian Patrol, alert for people to kick. Of course, nobody (neither manager nor worker) thinks about it that way, since it's so much a part of the corporate culture. But the thought of doing without it is inconceivable to many managers.

A recent consulting assignment involved taking part in a project to build a customer information system for a California company. The spec was written and we were ready to start blueprinting internal design. The boss called us all together and handed each person a map showing the way to an office in faraway Long Beach. He explained that there was a free conference room there where we could work uninterrupted. He would stay behind and fend off all but the most essential phone calls. We were told, "Come back when you're done." More than two weeks later, we came back with a hotshot design. He never called or dropped in once during the whole period.

—TRL

If you've got decent people under you, there is probably nothing you can do to improve their chances of success more dramatically than to get yourself out of their hair occasionally. Any easily separable task is a perfect opportunity. There is no real management required for such work. Send them away. Find a remote office, hire a conference room, borrow somebody's summer house, or put them up at a hotel. Take advantage of off-season rates at ski areas or at beaches. Have them go to a conference, and then stay over for a few days to work together in peace. (We've heard of at least one instance of each of these ploys.)

Such a plan will cost you some points with your own management and peers, because it's so audacious. How can you know, they'll ask you, that your people aren't loafing this very minute? How can you be sure they won't knock off for lunch at eleven and drink away their afternoons? The simple answer is you'll know by the product they come back with. By their fruits, ye shall know them. If they bring back a carefully thought-out and complete result, they worked. If they don't, they didn't. Visual supervision is a joke for development workers. Visual supervision is for prisoners.

Getting away from the office helps in many ways. First of all, it removes your highest-priced resources from the distractions and interruptions that fritter away so much of their time. You may succeed someday in building a productive office environment, a workplace where it's at least possible to get something useful done between 9 and 5. But you can only do this in the long run. In the short run, use any excuse to get your people out. In addition to making them more efficient, the getaway and the periods of total autonomy give them an improved chance to jell into a high-momentum team.

There Are Rules and We Do Break Them

The engineering profession is famous for a kind of development mode that doesn't exist elsewhere: the *skunkworks project*. *Skunkworks* implies that the project is hidden away someplace where it can be done without upper management's knowing what's going on. This happens when people at the lowest levels believe so strongly in the rightness of a product that they refuse to accept management's decision to kill it. Digital Equipment Corporation's PDP11, one of DEC's most successful products, came to the market in this manner. There is a lore about such projects. The amusing thing is that *skunkworks* is really just another word for *insubordination*. Management says no, and the project goes on anyway.

One of our clients tried to cancel a product that was judged to have no market. Cooler heads prevailed and the product was built. It became a huge success. The manager who had unsuccessfully tried to kill the project (he now had become president of the whole company) ordered a medal for the team, with the citation "First Annual Prize for Insubordination." He presented it with a speech, stating that others seeking the award had better be just as successful. Being an insubordinate failure wouldn't get anybody a prize.

People at all levels know whether some sensible insubordination is acceptable or not. People look out for their Open Kimono managers. They're determined to make them look good, even though the managers may botch an occasional decision. Defensive managers are on their own.

Chickens with Lips

In the mid-1970s, systems and organizational consultant Larry Constantine was counseling certain client companies to help them build a healthy corporate sociology. One of the things he advised was for the companies to allow people at the lowest level some voice in team selection. As implemented, the idea was that the company would post new projects on a central kiosk. People would form themselves into candidate teams and then "bid" on jobs. If you had a hankering to work with some of your mates, you would put your résumés together and make a joint pitch for the job. The points in your favor were how well-suited you were to the job, how well you complemented each other's capacities, and how little it would disrupt other work in the company to assign you as a group to this project. The company picked the best-suited team for each job.

This scheme gave people two unusual degrees of freedom: They got to choose the projects they worked on and the people they worked with. The surprising finding was that the first of these factors didn't matter very much. Management initially feared that only the glamorous projects would be bid for, but it didn't happen that way. Even the most mundane projects were bid for. What seemed to matter was the chance for people to work with those they wanted to work with.

The idea of an employment audition, presented in Chapter 16, "Hiring a Juggler," has a similar effect. The project members who listen to the audition are not just an audience; they have a say in whether the person gets the offer. In addition to technical judgment, they're supplying a team perspective on how well the candidate will fit in: "I think we could work with this guy," or "He seems well-qualified, but he'd stick out like a sore thumb in this group."

Some years ago, we were part of a pretty well-knit working group, a group whose members started to have many characteristics in common—in particular, a similar sense of humor. We even developed a shared theory about humor. This theory held that some things are intrinsically funny. Chickens, for instance, are funny, but horses aren't. Lips are hilarious, elbows and knees are funny, but shoulders are just shoulders. One day we had an audition for a new group member. After he'd spoken and left, one of our colleagues critiqued, "I guess you can't fault his knowledge. But do you think he'd ever come to understand that chickens with lips are funny?" The candidate didn't get the job.

Who's in Charge Here?

The best bosses take some chances. They take chances on their people. None of this says that good managers don't manage, that they don't give direction and make judgments of their own. They have to do this all the time. The suggestion here is that they do this only by exercising their *natural authority*. Between master craftsman and apprentice there is a bond of natural authority—the master knows how to do the work and the apprentice does not. Submitting to this kind of authority demeans no one, it doesn't remove incentive, it doesn't make it impossible to knit with fellow workers. An insecure need for obedience is the opposite of natural authority. It says, "Recognize me as a different caste of creature, a manager. I belong to the thinking class. Those beneath me are employed to carry out my decisions."

In the best organizations, there is natural authority working in all directions. The manager is known to be better at some things, perhaps setting general directions, negotiating, and hiring, and is trusted to do those things. Each of the workers is known to have some special area of expertise, and is trusted by all as a natural authority in that area. In this atmosphere of Open Kimono, the team has its optimal chance to jell.

28
Chemistry for Team Formation

Some organizations are famous for their consistent good luck in getting well-knit teams to happen. It isn't luck, of course; it's *chemistry*. There is something about those organizations, some optimal mix of competence and trust and mutual esteem and well-person sociology that provides perfect soil for the growth of jelled teams. And it's not only team formation that benefits from these factors. Everything works better. These organizations are just plain healthy.

Rather than illustrate this with an example from our experience, we encourage you to think of one from your own. Have you ever been in an organization that simply glowed with health? People were at ease, having a good time, and enjoying interactions with their peers. There was no defensiveness, no sense that single individuals were trying to succeed in spite of the efforts of those around them. The work was a joint product. Everybody was proud of its quality. (At least a glimmer of this healthy glow should be apparent in your present situation. If not, perhaps it's time to call in well, and get your résumé out.)

What are managers up to in these healthiest companies? A quick surface appraisal might convince you they aren't up to much at all. They don't seem busy. They're not giving a lot of directions. Whatever their relationship is to the work going on around them, they're certainly not *doing* any of it.

In organizations with the best chemistry, managers devote their energy to building and maintaining healthy chemistry. Departments and divisions that glow with health do so because their managers make it happen. There is a holistic integrity to their method, and so it's hard to break down and analyze the component parts (how the parts fit together into a whole is more important than what the parts are). But it's still worth a try.

167

Presented below is an admittedly simplistic list of the elements of a chemistry-building strategy for a healthy organization:

- Make a cult of quality.

- Provide lots of satisfying closure.

- Build a sense of eliteness.

- Allow and encourage heterogeneity.

- Preserve and protect successful teams.

- Provide strategic but not tactical direction.

There are more. We've cited only those elements that have a particular effect on team formation. The following subsections provide our comments on each of these points.

The Cult of Quality

The judgment that a still-imperfect product is "good enough" is the death knell for a jelling team. There can be no impetus to bind together with your cohorts for the joint satisfaction gained from delivering mediocre work. The opposite attitude, of "only perfect is good enough for us," gives the team a real chance. This cult of quality is the strongest catalyst for team formation.

It binds the team together because it sets its members apart from the rest of the world. The rest of the world, remember, doesn't give a hoot for quality. Oh, it talks a good game, but if quality costs a nickel extra, you quickly see the true colors of those who would have to shell out the nickel.

Our friend Lou Mazzucchelli, one of the founders of Cadre Technologies, Inc., was in the market for a paper shredder. He had a salesman come in to demonstrate a unit. It was a disaster. It was enormous and noisy (it made a racket even when it wasn't shredding). Our friend asked about a German-made shredder he'd heard about. The salesman was contemptuous. It cost nearly half again as much and didn't have a single extra feature, he responded. "All you get for that extra money," he said, "is better quality."

Your marketplace, your product consumers, your clients, and your upper management are never going to make the case for high quality. Extraordinary quality doesn't make good short-term economic sense. When team members develop a cult of quality, they always turn out something that's better than what their market is asking for. They can do this, but only when protected from short-term economics. In the long run, this always pays off. People get high on quality and outdo themselves to protect it.

The cult of quality works like the grain of sand in an oyster; it is a focal point for the team to bind around.

I Told Her I Loved Her When I Married Her

It may be news to some, but the human creature needs reassurance from time to time that he or she is headed in the right direction. Teams of human creatures need it, too. Such reassurance comes from what psychologists call *closure*. Closure is the satisfying "thunk" of pieces of the whole falling into place.

Organizations also have some need for closure. Closure for the organization is the successful finish of the work as assigned, plus perhaps an occasional confirmation along the way that everything is on target (maybe a milestone achieved or a significant partial delivery completed). How much confirmation corporations require is a function of how much money is at risk. Sometimes, closure only at the end of a four-year effort is adequate for the needs of the organization.

The problem here is that organizations have far less need for closure than do the people who work for them. The prospect of four years of work without any satisfying "thunk" leaves everyone in the group thinking, "I could be dead before this thing is ever done." Particularly when the team is coming together, frequent closure is important. Team members need to get into the habit of succeeding together and liking it. This is part of the mechanism by which the team builds momentum.

The chemistry-building manager takes pains to divide the work into pieces and makes sure that each piece has some substantive demonstration of its own completion. Such a manager may contrive to deliver a product in twenty versions, even though two are sufficient for upper management and the user. It may even be necessary to conceal some of these interim versions from the client, and build them only for internal confirmation and satisfaction. Each new version is an opportunity for closure. Team members get warmed up as the moment approaches; they sprint near the very end. They get a high from success. It suffuses them with renewed energy for the next step. It makes them feel closer together.

The Elite Team

In the early 1970s, a vice president of one of our client companies sent around a memo on the subject of travel expenses to everyone in his division. You may have received similar memos on the topic yourself, but this one was different. It said more or less this: "It has come to my attention that some of you, when traveling on expenses, have been traveling economy class. This is not an economy-class organization. This is a first-class organization. When you fly on business from now on, you will fly first class." Of course, that memo cost money. The expense was very real and the only thing you could balance against it was an enhanced sense of eliteness. At least one organization thought that was a valid trade-off. Couldn't happen in a real-world corporation, you say? It happened at Xerox.

Those who think popcorn is "unprofessional" think team eliteness is downright subversive. There is a widespread feeling that managers are just not doing their jobs if the team sticks out in any way. The group's adherence to a corporate standard of uniformity is almost a symbol of the manager's degree of control. Yet from the viewpoint of the people being managed, this symbol is deadly. The more comforting it is to the manager, the more it saps the lifeblood of the team.

People require a sense of uniqueness to be at peace with themselves, and they need to be at peace with themselves to let the jelling process begin. When management acts to stifle uniqueness, uniqueness happens anyway. People simply express their uniqueness in uncontrolled dimensions. For example, employees who take a perverse pride in being difficult to manage or hard to motivate or unable to work with others may be reacting to too much control. They would almost certainly rather express themselves in some less difficult way, something that would not work to the detriment of the group's effectiveness.

What could be wrong with a team that is uniquely quality-conscious or uniquely productive or uniquely competent to meet a tough deadline? Nothing, you might think, yet even these nominally acceptable forms of uniqueness are upsetting to lots of managers. They grumble that the teams are unmanageable and uppity. What's really threatened by the team's eliteness is not manageability, but the trappings of managerial strength. The team might be hell-bent on success, but the manager is worried about being considered a wimp.

If you could effect some change in the people you manage and make them much more productive and goal-directed but also less controllable, would you do it? The answer to this question distinguishes the great managers from the merely mediocre. The mediocre manager is too insecure to give up the trappings. The great manager knows that people can't be controlled in any meaningful sense anyway. The essence of successful management is to get everyone pulling in the same direction and then somehow get them fired up to the point that nothing, not even their manager, could stop their progress.

A jelled team does have the effect of making people more productive and goal-directed. And you do give up some control, or at least the illusion of control, when it jells. The team begins to feel elite in some way or other, with all members of the team sharing in the sense of eliteness. The unique thing about the team doesn't have to be anything very fundamental. For example, there was one championship football defensive unit whose only unique characteristic was that all members of the team were "no-names." It was enough. They took pride in that fact and knit around it. Whatever the elite characteristic is, it forms the basis of the team's identity, and identity is an essential ingredient of a jelled team.

An important qualifier here is that teams need to be unique in some sense, but not in all senses. There are lots of examples of teams that comply with institutional standards of appearance. Military specialty teams and most sports teams dress alike. But as long as they are allowed to feel unique in some sense, they can conform in others.

Managers who feel threatened by elite teams often talk of the deleterious effect their eliteness can have on people outside the team. If members of one small working group begin to characterize themselves as Winners, isn't everyone else automatically put into the category Losers? It is true that extremely successful teams can be daunting to those outside the team. But this is not so much the effect of the team as of the success. If this is your only problem, you should be writing your own book.

On Not Breaking Up the Yankees

If a team does knit, don't break it up. At least give people the option to undertake another project together. They may choose to go their separate ways, but they ought to have the choice. When teams stay together from one project to the next, they start out each new endeavor with enormous momentum.

A Network Model of Team Behavior

This may offend your sensibilities as a manager, but managers are usually not part of the teams that they manage. Teams are made up of peers, equals that function as equals. The manager is most often outside the team, giving occasional direction from above and clearing away administrative and procedural obstacles. By definition, the manager is not a peer and so can't be part of the peer group.

This idea is upsetting to managers who pride themselves on their leadership. Isn't the manager supposed to supply leadership, to function as quarterback, spiriting the team on to victory through judicious play selection and split-second timing? That may sound good, but the team that needs that much leadership isn't functioning very well as a team. On the best teams, different individuals provide occasional leadership, taking charge in areas where they have particular strengths. No one is the permanent leader, because that person would then cease to be a peer and the team interaction would begin to break down.

The structure of a team is a network, not a hierarchy. For all the deference paid to the concept of *leadership* (a cult word in our industry), it just doesn't have much place here.

Selections from a Chinese Menu

In writing about teams, we have traded somewhat on the easy analogy between teams in industry and teams in sports. The very word *team* conjures up an image of healthy young folks sweatily pursuing footballs or hockey pucks or each other. It's hard to think about teams without reference to sports, but the sports analogy carries some unfortunate baggage.

The typical team you see thrashing away on weekend television is made up of individuals with a lot in common: Members of a basketball team, for instance, may all be tall, young, strong, and of the same sex. They're alike because the nature of their endeavor requires that they be alike. There is less of a requirement for sameness on development project teams. But since our whole notion of teams is affected by the sports example, we often expect sameness on the team and perhaps unwittingly bring it about.

A little bit of heterogeneity can be an enormous aid to create a jelled team. Add one handicapped developer to a newly formed work group, and the odds go up that the team will knit. The same effect can result from adding a co-op student or an ex-admin on the first project after being retrained. Whatever the heterogeneous element is, it takes on symbolic importance to team members. It is a clear signal that it's okay not to be a clone, okay not to fit into the corporate mold of Uniform Plastic Person.

The saddest example of the overly homogeneous work group is the all-male team. Of course, women function as well on teams as men. Any man who has worked on mixed teams would find it hard to imagine ever again working in the all-male environment. That was our grandfathers' sad lot.

Putting It All Together

You can't always make it happen, but when a team does come together, it's worth the cost. The work is fun; the people are energized. They roll over deadlines and milestones and look for more. They like themselves. They feel loyal to the team and to the environment that allows the team to exist.

PART V

Fertile Soil

Projects and teams exist within a context provided by the larger organization. We call this context the corporate culture. Some cultures support healthy work, while others may make it almost impossible. While factors at the organizational level might be beyond your ability to control, they're still worth considering. At worst, you need to be aware of what's being imposed upon you from above; at best, you may someday be in a position to revamp it to best facilitate the work going on in projects underneath you.

29

The Self-Healing System

An employee storms into the Personnel Department and resigns. The next morning, he and his boss turn up to explain rather sheepishly that the whole thing was a silly mistake. Would it be possible to undo his resignation? The workers handling the case look at the partly completed transaction in some perplexity. Whoever had designed the procedures for dealing with termination had made no allowance for undoing. But it's easy enough to see what will make it all come out right: Let's see, we can just drop this whole file into the wastebasket and pretend it never existed, then we void out the final payroll check and run over to Harry's desk and grab the insurance cancellation forms before he sees them. . . .

A system has just healed itself. Something had been left out of its original design, something that turned out to be necessary. The people who make the system go have fixed it on the fly. It happens all the time.

Deterministic and Nondeterministic Systems

When you automate a previously all-human system, it becomes entirely deterministic. The new system is capable of making only those responses planned explicitly by its builders. So the self-healing quality is lost. Any response that will be required must be put there in the first place. If ever the system needs to be healed, that can only be done outside the context of its operation. Maintainers come in to take the system apart and reconstruct it with one or more new planned responses added.

In one view, getting rid of the rather messy and uncontrollable self-healing capacity is a positive benefit of automation. The system is planned "right" in the first place, and then there is no need for tinkering during operation. But it's no secret that this can be expensive. Automators spend much of their time thinking through situations that are so unlikely or occur so rarely that the human elements of the old system never even bothered to consider them unless and until they actually happened. If the business policy governing the new system has a sufficient degree of natural ad hoc-racy, it's a mistake to automate it. Determinism will be no asset then; the system will be in constant need of maintenance.

The reason that nondeterministic systems can often heal themselves painlessly and elegantly (sometimes at no cost at all) is that the humans who make up the system have an easy familiarity with the underlying goals. When a new situation crops up, they know immediately what action makes sense. Someday it may be possible to teach computers the goals of the system instead of the actions expected to achieve the goals, but right now that's beyond the horizon. The point here is that making a system deterministic will result in the loss of its ability to heal itself.

The organization that you work in or manage is in some sense a system. It is an amalgam of interacting people and processes that exist to achieve some end. It's all the vogue these days to talk of making such systems more deterministic. That brings us to the subject of Methodology.

The Covert Meaning of Methodology

The maddening thing about most of our organizations is that they are only as good as the people who staff them. Wouldn't it be nice if we could get around that natural limit, and have good organizations even though they were staffed by mediocre or incompetent people? Nothing could be easier—all we need is (trumpet fanfare, please) a Methodology.

A Methodology is a general systems theory of how a whole class of thought-intensive work ought to be conducted. It comes in the form of a fat book that specifies in detail exactly what steps to take at any time, regardless of who's doing the work, regardless of where or when. The people who write the Methodology are smart. The people who carry it out can be dumb. They never have to turn their brains to the ON position. All they do is start on page one and follow the Yellow Brick Road, like happy little Munchkins, all the way from the start of the job to its successful completion. The Methodology makes all the decisions; the people make none. The organization becomes entirely deterministic.

Like any other system, a team of human workers will lose its self-healing properties to the extent it becomes deterministic. The result can be workers proceeding in directions that make no sense to them at all, a sure sign that they can't be doing any good. Some years ago, we conducted a postmortem of a failed project by asking each of the project workers to record observations about the project. They did this in the privacy of their own homes and we assured them that only we two, the consultants, would ever see their responses. One of the project workers gave us this observation:

> *By March, we had been doing this [applying one of the techniques dictated from on high] for nearly two months. I couldn't see how it was helping us in any way, but George kept assuring us that it was. He said we should trust in the Methodology, and it would all work out in the end.*

Of course, it didn't. The project workers are the ones most familiar with the territory of the project. If a given direction doesn't make sense to them, *it doesn't make any sense at all.*

There is a big difference between Methodology and methodology. Small *m* methodology is a basic approach one takes to getting a job done. It doesn't reside in a fat book, but rather inside the heads of the people carrying out the work. Such a methodology consists of two parts: a tailored plan (specific to the work at hand) and a body of skills necessary to effect the plan. One could hardly be opposed to methodology: The work couldn't even begin without it. But a Methodology is very different

Big *M* Methodology is an attempt to centralize thinking.[1] All meaningful decisions are made by the Methodology builders, not by the staff assigned to do the work. Those who espouse a Methodology have a long list of its supposed benefits, including standardization, documentary uniformity, managerial control, and state-of-the-art techniques. These make up the overt case for the Methodology. The covert case is simpler and cruder: the idea that project people aren't smart enough to do the thinking.

Methodology Madness

Of course, if your people aren't smart enough to think their way through their work, the work will fail. No Methodology will help. Worse still, Methodologies

---

1. In the software development field, *Methodology* suddenly became a bad word and people started talking instead about *Process*. (Let us know if you ever detect any difference.)

can do grievous damage to efforts in which the people are fully competent. They do this by trying to force the work into a fixed mold that guarantees

- A morass of paperwork
- A paucity of methods
- An absence of responsibility
- A general loss of motivation

The following paragraphs comment on each of these effects.

Paperwork: The Methodologies themselves are huge and getting huger (they have to grow to add the "features" required by each new kind of situation). It's not at all unusual for a Methodology to use up a linear foot or more of shelf space. Worse, they encourage people to build documents rather than do work. The documentary obsession of such Methodologies seems to have resulted from paranoid defensive thinking along these lines: "The last project generated a ton of paper and it was still a disaster, so this project will have to generate two tons." The technological sectors of our economy have now been through a decades-long flirtation with the idea that more and more and more paperwork will solve its problems. Perhaps it's time to introduce this contrary and heretical notion:

> *Voluminous documentation is part of the problem, not part of the solution.*

Methods: The centerpiece of most Methodologies is the concept of standardized methods. If there were a thousand different but equally good ways to go about the work, it might make some sense to choose one and standardize upon it. But in our state of technological infancy, there are very few competing methods for most of the work we do. When there are genuine alternatives, people have to know about and master them all. To standardize on one is to exclude the others. It boils down to the view that knowledge is so valuable, we must use it sparingly.

Responsibility: If something goes wrong on a Methodology effort, the fault is with the Methodology, not the people. (The Methodology, after all, made all of the decisions.) Working in such an environment is virtually responsibility-free. People want to accept responsibility, but they won't unless given acceptable degrees of freedom to control their own success.

Motivation: The message in the decision to impose a Methodology is apparent to all. Nothing could be more demotivating than the knowledge that management thinks its workers incompetent.

The Issue of Malicious Compliance

Those who build Methodologies are tortured by the thought that thinking people will simply ignore them. In many organizations, that is just what happens. Even more upsetting is the opposite possibility: that people won't ignore the Methodology, but will instead do *exactly* what it says to do, even when they know doing so will lead to wasted time, unworkable products, and meaningless documentation. This is what our colleague Ken Orr calls "malicious compliance." When the Methodology calls for an 18-part operator's manual, developers may write one, even for a product so deeply imbedded in an engine or a satellite that no operator intervention is possible. When the Methodology says you have to fill out a database residency form for each data element, developers may do so, even though the system has no database.

In Australia, where striking uses up nearly as much labor time as working, there is a charming form of strike called *work to rule*. Rather than walk off the job, workers open up a fat book of procedures and announce, "Until you give us what we're asking for, we're going to work exactly to the rule." When the air-traffic controllers do this, for instance, they can only land one plane every seven minutes. If doctors were to do it, an appendectomy would take a week. Introduction of a Methodology opens up the possibility of work-to-rule actions in still more parts of the economy. People might actually do exactly what the Methodology says, and the work would grind nearly to a halt.

The Baby and the Bathwater

Most of the benefits claimed on behalf of Methodologies are really benefits of convergence of method. To the extent that different people doing the same work converge on the same methods and use them the same way, there can be real advantages. Maintenance personnel will be able to relate more quickly to new products, developers will be able to move onto new projects and get up to speed more quickly, metrics will be consistently defined from one effort to another, and certain kinds of failures will be more readily detectable. Convergence of method is a good thing. But Methodologies are not the only way to achieve convergence.

Methodologies seek to force convergence through statute. There is an inevitable backlash, the result partly of enforcers' heavy-handedness and partly of thinking workers' strong sense of independence, the cowboy mentality so common to those who populate any new frontier. Better ways to achieve convergence of method are

> **Training:** People do what they know how to do. If you give them all a common core of methods, they will tend to use those methods.

> **Tools:** A few automated aids for modeling, design, implementation, and test will get you more convergence of method than all the statutes you can pass.

> **Peer Review:** In organizations where there are active peer-review mechanisms (quality circles, walkthroughs, inspections, technology fairs), there is a natural tendency toward convergence.

It's only after this kind of gently guided convergence that you may think of publishing a standard. You can't really declare something a standard until it has already become a de facto standard. This is fundamental to the theory of standardization at DuPont, for instance. That company's standards manual during the years we consulted there defined a standard as "a proven method for undertaking a repeated task." The manual went on to explain that *proven* means "demonstrated widely and successfully within DuPont." That seems like common sense to us, but it goes against the industry-wide convention of hunting out new approaches and imposing them as standards before anyone in the organization has even tried them out.

The High-Tech Illusion Revisited

The obsession with Methodologies in the workplace is another instance of the High-Tech Illusion. It stems from the belief that what really matters is the technology. Even the best imaginable Methodology, one that prescribes exactly the right method for every activity, may give only a small improvement in the technology. The people, after all, aren't going to make every decision wrong, even without guidance. Whatever the technological advantage may be, it may come only at the price of a significant worsening of the team's sociology.

The opposite approach would be one in which every new undertaking is run as a pilot project. To the extent that there was a standard way to carry out the work, that would be the only way you *weren't* allowed to carry it out. The standard would be for at least one part of the effort to be run in a non-standard way. (This seems to be an informal rule within certain divisions of Fujitsu, for instance.)

In the spring of 1932, efficiency experts ran a series of tests at the Hawthorne Western Electric Company to determine the effects of various environmental parameters on productivity. They tried raising the light level, and they noted that productivity went up. Then they tried lowering the light level, and they noted that productivity went up higher still. They speculated that turning the lights off entirely might send productivity through the roof. What seemed to be happening was that the change itself wasn't as important as the act of changing. People were charmed by differentness, they liked the attention, they were intrigued by novelty. This has come to be called the *Hawthorne Effect*. Loosely stated, it says that people perform better when they're trying something new.

A careful study of the literature of productivity improvement could convince you that all productivity improvements are due to the Hawthorne Effect. Invariably, a paper that touts the wonderful benefits of X is reporting on productivity gains when X was first introduced. You almost never hear of a study that analyzes ten-year-old "improvements" to see if they are still worthwhile. They probably aren't. With only a modicum of cynicism, we subscribe to the view that the Hawthorne Effect accounts for most productivity gains.

To allow the Hawthorne Effect to work for you, you have to make non-standard approaches the rule. Whatever standard there is should be brief and gentle. The total of all standards imposed upon your people should be described in no more than ten pages. (This is no pipe dream; many organizations that have given up on the Methodology-as-Law approach end up with ten-page standards manuals.) You ought to be prepared to grant exceptions to even this loose guide. This gives you a development environment consistent with the views of that famous business sage Mao Tse-tung:

> Let a hundred flowers blossom and
> let a hundred schools of thought contend.

Of course, Mao didn't really mean it, but we do.

30
Dancing with Risk

Our book *Waltzing With Bears: Managing Risk on Software Projects* takes issue with two opposite kinds of behavior: risk-taking without risk management, and risk-aversion that makes impossible the accomplishment of anything ambitious. What we now see in increasing numbers are organizations that manage to err on both sides: They take on one class of stupid risk with impunity, while avoiding the very ones that might be indicators of transformational value.

The Peopleware premise—our main problems are more likely to be sociological than technological in nature—applies nowhere more strongly than in the area of risk. The mechanics of risk management are widely understood; when it doesn't get done, the reason is likely to be in the organization's politics and culture.

Not Running Away from Risk

First of all, it's worth saying that project risk is a good thing, a likely indicator of value. Projects that have real value but little or no risk were all done ages ago. The ones that matter today are laden with risk.

Imagine that you were hired to run the project that Barnes & Noble undertook to create software support for its Nook e-reader. This is what you're up against: Your principal competition, Amazon, has simply run away with the market; you are very late in getting started; your device has no particular advantage over theirs (same underlying technology); you're barely started making deals with the publishers for electronic rights, and you're probably never going to catch up anyway with the number of books Amazon can already offer. What do you do?

What the benighted souls who were actually in that position did was to take a huge risk. They decided to offer something that the competition had not even thought of yet: library borrowing of e-publications. But think about what's involved to make that work: negotiations not just with publishers, but with libraries and authors as well; establishing and implementing protocols for the borrowing network; building software into the reader to make books expire when the borrowing period is up; a royalty system to reward authors of borrowed books. Risk, risk, and more risk. And coupled with the risks of navigating those uncharted waters, there is also the risk that the market will just say ho-hum. Who knows how much appeal borrowing is likely to have?

The risks paid off in this case. The Nook was delivered with its surprising differentiator, and the market took to it.

Think about what your risk list would have looked like on that project. There were lots of things that could have gone wrong along the way, and managing them would have been a major part of your job. If you made up—off the top of your head—a quick list of all those risks, we bet there's one important one you might have left out.

The One Risk We Almost Never Manage

The risk we tend not to manage is the risk of our own failure. If you and your trusted team have to interact with a contractor from thousands of miles and ten time zones away in a city you've never heard of, of course you put their possible nonperformance at the top of your risk list. That's obvious. But how about the risk that you and your own team won't meet *your* portion of the assigned goals? Of course, you worry about that; you may wake up at night in a sweat over it. The reason it might not make your risk list is that it looks like defeatism to carry a risk of your own nonperformance. After all, you've been entrusted to assure performance; it's your assigned responsibility.

To understand why not managing even this one risk is dangerous, you need to consider the real reason for risk management: It's not to make the risks go away, but to enable sensible mitigation should they occur. And mitigation may well have to be planned and provisioned well ahead of time.

The infamous Denver International Airport Baggage Handling System is a case in point. The powers that be had decided that on-time delivery of the system was so important that nonperformance (lateness) could not be considered a risk. It wasn't a risk because it simply wasn't going to be allowed to happen. The risk was whisked away by managerial fiat.

If they had managed the risk, they would have been obliged to plan a manual or semi-automatic backup plan to move the bags in case the new system wasn't ready. They didn't. So when the system was late, they had to defer opening the airport. The capital cost of carrying a second nonfunctional airport for more than a year eventually came to billions.

By the time the risk materialized and the system wasn't available on opening day, it was too late to start mitigation planning. If, on the other hand, the mitigation had been ready, the airport would have opened with old-fashioned, temporary guys-plus-little-trucks moving the baggage, and the lateness of the software system would have been nothing more than a minor disappointment. You never would have heard of DIA's Baggage Handling System; no one would have except the people on the project.

It's perfectly reasonable not to manage a risk for which the probability of occurrence is extremely low. It's not reasonable to leave unmanaged the risk for which the consequences are "just too awful to think about."

Why Nonperformance Risks Often Don't Get Managed

Can-do thinking often replaces risk management when the outcome has been defined as a challenge. People rise to a challenge; they welcome it. They get genned up to prove themselves against adversity. The last thing they need is to spend any of their time planning and provisioning for their own failure. Time is of the essence, especially when the challenge is to get something done on a tight schedule. The more the schedule matters, the less time for mitigation planning and the less people are inclined to do it.

This need not be all bad. If the manager and his or her team aren't going to do risk management, someone else has to. The best project manager in this situation is the one who can say, "Look, we're willing to take on this challenge, this scary delivery date, and we'll do our best to meet it. We'll have no time to manage the risk that we won't make it in spite of our best efforts, but somebody better manage that risk. Unless we see that specific plans are being made for the eventuality of our late delivery, we're not going to be able to think of this as a challenge; it's more of a stupid, desperation crapshoot."

Middle-level managers and executives are often skilled at characterizing a desired outcome as a challenge. They pose the challenge as something that will be a proof of excellence. But in many cases what they're trying to accomplish is not to goad the team into excellence, but to get team members to finish the project on the cheap. Perversely, the more marginal the benefit carried by the project, the more important it is to deliver it cheaply. It's no surprise that cheap delivery to hide lousy benefit is not a great motivator, so executives in this position might find themselves saying, "This work is so important that we must have it done by January first." What they really mean is, "This work is so *unimportant* that we don't want to fund it beyond January first."

This is a false challenge, but the team and team leader may not understand it as such. They may sign on to the aggressive delivery date and do their best to meet it, shedding all pretense of risk management on the way.

False challenge projects always have the same characteristics: marginal benefit (since they take on no real technological risk because the organization is risk-averse), but huge schedule risk that is typically unmanaged. Welcome to the worst of both worlds.

31

Meetings, Monologues, and Conversations

Some organizations are so addicted to meetings that work has to take second place. They hold meetings that have little purpose and no clearly defined end-state. At the other extreme, some organizations are so fearful of the waste of meetings that they refuse to use the "M" word at all. This, too, has its downside. The middle is the only safe ground.

Neuro-sclerosis

As organizations age, meeting time increases until—in the final stages—there is time for nothing else. At least it seems that way. There are reasons why this happens, often good ones, but the effect can still be so drastically slowing that the competition can be faintly heard rejoicing in the distance. As the number of vested parties to any action increases, meeting population goes up. Additionally, meetings give visibility, an essential factor to anyone who hopes to rise in big-company hierarchy. You don't get noticed by listening thoughtfully, so anyone who's there for visibility is likely to be a talker. The worst meetings feel like congregations of windbags with nobody listening and everybody speaking or waiting to speak. Because there are so many who need to speak, meeting duration increases seemingly without bound.

While everyone deplores the time used up by these meetings, lots of managers excuse them as an unfortunate necessity: necessary because of the monumental complexity of what the organization is trying to do. The notion of monumental complexity, of course, confers status on everyone, so once it has been advanced as justification for the meetings, nobody is very inclined to offer the alternate possibility: competitive windbagging.

The "Technologically Enhanced" Meeting

Enter technology. While our predecessors had to endure bad meetings without any means of release, we have our connected laptops. We can open them up when things get dull, . . . oops, that might be unwise—better just open them up at the beginning of each meeting so as not to send a signal when Harry gets up that all of us are drifting away.

So now, the dull meeting is a chance to deal with the flood of e-mails waiting in the In-box or maybe to take a quick peek at a few Facebook pages or to send a text to some other poor bastard who's trapped here, too, sitting on the other side of the table. Or, even to do a bit of work . . .

Now that we've noted what the enhancing technology can do for you, let's ask the parallel question: What has it done for the meeting? Made it better, right? More effective, more efficient. Get serious. Sure, there may come a moment in a meeting when some manager suggests, "One of you with an open laptop, nip out to the Internet to get us some figures about how big this market sector we're talking about [at least the one that he's talking about] is this year and how it's projected to grow in the near future." That *can* happen. Just not very often. For every fetch of information that is actually germane to what the meeting is supposed to be about, there are probably a thousand that are completely unrelated.

Here's the rub: The technology that is so evident at meetings today does not facilitate the meeting at all; it merely provides an escape for people from the pointlessness of what's happening around them. What the technology enhances is the dreadfulness of meetings. Our meetings are worse today than they were a generation ago, because a generation ago people wouldn't have been able to bear them—they would have revolted.

Behavior that we take for granted today would have gotten you fired a generation ago.

Stand-Up Meetings

A somewhat new wrinkle is the stand-up meeting, typically conducted in an empty space (no tables or chairs) with all participants on their feet. The theory is that no one gets too comfortable and so the tendency to prattle on is reduced. Makes sense to us, but in our cynical view the great benefit of the stand-up is that nobody has a surface to place a laptop on, so they all stay closed. Whatever the cause, the meetings tend to be shorter, and that's a plus.

Even short stand-ups can be a drag on an organization's effectiveness if they lack purpose and focus. So what should the purpose and focus of a meeting be? That's going to depend on what kind of a meeting it is.

Basic Meeting Hygiene

A meeting that is specifically called to get something done might be called a *working meeting*. (The others, you might assume, are *nonworking* meetings. More about them in the next section.) A working meeting is typically called to reach a decision. Who should be invited? That's easy, the people who need to agree before the decision can be judged made. Nobody else. To make sure no one is blindsided, it's essential that the working meeting have an agenda relevant to its purpose and that it stick to that agenda. Thus, no one risks anything by not attending because they come to have confidence that off-agenda matters won't be discussed. No one has to attend defensively.

Working meetings have a charming characteristic. You know when they're done. When the decision has been reached, there is no further need to meet. Before it's been reached, the meeting is not yet complete.

Same idea backwards: If you can say definitively what group action terminates the meeting, then it's a working meeting. If you can't, it isn't.

If you apply this test to the next meeting you attend, you'll almost certainly conclude it isn't a working meeting. It isn't because no result of the group interaction ends the meeting. What ends the meeting is the clock. It's 10 A.M., so the meeting is over.

Ceremonies

A meeting that is ended by the clock is a *ceremony*. Its purpose is not to get any particular thing decided. It's all FYI. The FYIing often happens in a ritualistic manner: quick intro and announcements by a boss, followed by serial one-on-one interactions between the boss and each subordinate. At any given moment, two people are involved. The others are nominally listening, with emphasis on the nominally. If they have their laptops open, their focus is somewhere else.

The ceremony is a series of conversations, and conversations are a good thing. What's not such a good thing is all the non-listeners locked in the room while the conversations take place. Those who believe that meetings should be replaced with conversations observe that the one-on-ones might just as well take place somewhere else with all the rest of the participants released to do real work.

There is occasionally a real need for ceremony in the workplace. A ceremony might be called to celebrate some accomplishment, to lay out a strategic change of direction, or to evaluate a project at its end. All of these justifiable ceremonies are a bit out of the ordinary. That's what makes them justifiable. It's the regular ceremony that needs to be suspect. An example of a regular ceremony is the weekly (or daily!) status meeting, with ten or twenty people locked in a room taking turns talking to the boss.

Too Many People

The attendance of working meetings is limited to the vested-interest participants, the fewer the better. The attendance of ceremonial meetings is not limited at all. Anybody that the person in charge deems desirable is going to be there, the more the merrier. The importance of the meeting caller is reflected in the size of the group, so the incentive is to make it large.

The fantasy of "open organization" makes it worse.

My new client, viewed from the outside, looked like a sprightly young technology start-up, maybe a future generation's Apple. On the inside, it looked very different. At the meeting where I was introduced, every single manager was present. I thought they were all there because of me, and was duly flattered. But a succession of meetings over the next few days were the same: all managers present. One of the things that tended to happen at the meetings (no matter what the nominal subject was) was for staff to be moved around from project to project. No managers dared miss a meeting for fear that their people would be pinched. They excused the over-attendance by explaining proudly that they were an open organization. The real explanation was defensive participation.

—TDM

This is just basic math, but worth saying: The cost of the meeting is directly proportional to the number attending. One of our clients, an Apple manager, makes a point of releasing at least one person at the start of each meeting. She allows the released person a chance to make a quick statement. She makes it clear that her choice of who gets released is not the person's relative uselessness, rather it is the importance of the work he or she will be doing instead of sitting in. The savings of a single person released are probably not huge, but the message the release sends is hard to miss.

Open-Space Networking

If you've ever attended a professional conference or congress, you've probably come to the same conclusion as everyone else: The sessions and paper presentations can be a chore, while the real value of the experience is in the interstices, the common areas before and after each talk, the coffee breaks, the lunch lines, drinks and/or dinner with the other attendees. With this in mind, some ingenious person hit upon the idea of "open space." An Open-Space conference is essentially all coffee break and lunch. It's a bit more complicated than that, but you get the idea. There are no formal sessions; it's all about networking.

The same idea can be useful in meeting planning. As a new employee of an organization that is into Open-Space meetings, your experience of it might be something like this: You get a note from your boss announcing a staff meeting at 9 A.M. on Friday. You show up at 8:30, grab a coffee, and sit down with one of the new people you've just met to pick up on the prior day's conversation. Someone else joins your conversation and introductions are made. She is aware of what you've been assigned and tells you something of her own experience in the area.

The boss is now in the room and you wander over to show that you're there. He introduces you to a worker from an allied project using the same hardware you've been assigned to. The two of you exchange e-mail addresses and agree to get together for a working lunch later the same day. You overhear a conversation about something that has always fascinated you and you edge closer to hear more, wondering if the participants will clam up in the presence of a stranger. They don't. They gather you in, make introductions, and catch you up on what they'd been saying.

It's now well after 9, but the meeting still hasn't been called to order. You head to the buffet table to get another coffee and pause there to chat with someone from the support team. At last, at 9:20, the boss claps for attention, and says, "This has been great. Thank you, everyone, for coming. See you next week—same time, same place." Then he leaves. . . .

You've just had your first Open-Space experience. There was no real meeting, just one big interstice.

Prescription for Curing a Meeting-Addicted Organization

You can't change the world above you, but you can change your own area and the lives of the people who work beside and below you. The changes are easy to describe but hard to effect. Your goal should be to eliminate most ceremonial meetings and spend the time in one-on-one conversation, to limit attendance at working meetings and apply the "What ends this meeting?" test to each one. In place of ceremonies, encourage Open-Space networking to give people a chance to have unstructured interaction. Most important, curtail your own need for the confirmation that is provided by ceremonial meetings.

32

The Ultimate Management
Sin Is . . .

The ultimate management sin is wasting people's time. It sounds like this should be an easy sin to avoid, but it isn't. You have some needs of your own as a manager, and these needs may run squarely against your intention to preserve and use wisely the time of the people working under you.

For Instance

You call a meeting with your staff but arrive late yourself (you had to take an urgent call from your own boss), leaving the others to cool their heels. Or, you let yourself be called out of the meeting for a quick but important chat with the client, and the meeting loses focus without you. Or, you call a meeting and it becomes evident that the meeting itself is a waste of everyone's time (except possibly your own, the characteristic of many ceremonial meetings).

When you convoke a meeting with n people present, the normal presumption is that all those in the room are there because they need to interact with each other in order to come to certain conclusions. When, instead, the participants take turns interacting with one key figure, the expected rationale for assembling the whole group is missing; the boss might just as well have interacted separately with each of the subordinates without obliging the others to listen in.

We stated above that it may have been the boss's need that was being served, perhaps at the expense of some of the subordinates' time. But isn't this okay? Isn't this what bosses have to do in order to keep control? Isn't this a legitimate cost of managing and coordinating complex efforts? Yes and no. The meeting wasn't really necessary to convey status; there are many less wasteful ways to do that. The need that was being served was not the boss's need for information, but for *reassurance*. The ceremony supplies reassurance. It establishes for everyone that the boss is boss, that he or she gets to run the meeting, that attendance is expected, that the hierarchy is being respected.

Status Meetings Are About Status

A real working meeting is called when there is a real reason for *all* the people invited to think through some matter together. The purpose of the meeting is to reach consensus. Such a meeting is, almost by definition, an ad hoc affair. Ad hoc implies that the meeting is unlikely to be regularly scheduled. Any regular get-together is therefore somewhat suspect as likely to have a ceremonial purpose rather than a focused goal of consensus. The weekly status meeting is an obvious example. Though its goal may seem to be status reporting, its real intent is status confirming. And it's not the status of the work, but the status of the boss.

When bosses are particularly needy, the burden of ceremonial status meetings can grow almost without bound. We know of one organization, for example, that runs daily two-hour status meetings. When participants are off-site during a meeting, they are expected to call in and participate by speakerphone for the whole duration. Nonattendance is regarded as a threat and is subject to serious penalties.

Early Overstaffing

Meetings are not the only way that people's time gets wasted. When staff is brought on too quickly at the beginning of a project, there is almost always a waste of people's time. Again, you might think this is an easy sin to avoid: Just figure out how quickly the work can absorb new people; then bring them on, only at that rate. Although this makes perfectly good sense, it is often politically infeasible.

Projects begin with planning and design, activities that are best carried out by a smallish team. When design is important (as it is for anything but a simple formula project), it can require as much as half the full project duration. This suggests an ideal staffing plan that resembles Figure 32–1.

For a two-year project, the bulk of the staff would not come on board until the project is six months to a year underway. But so what? The staffing plan looks a little unusual, but if that's what's called for, why not staff it just that way?

Figure 32-1   Looks odd, but may be the ideal.

The problem makes itself apparent when the project is under a time constraint—and what project isn't? If the client and upper management have decreed, for example, that only a year is allowed for the work, then that limit will truncate the expected end of the project (see Figure 32-2).

There is a natural inclination to take the effort lopped off the end and apply it back at the beginning. Voilà, a project with this familiar pattern of early overstaffing (Figure 32-3).

Of course, if you knew the early added effort would just be wasted, you wouldn't do that, would you? Well, perhaps you would. You may conclude that your chances of finishing on such an aggressive schedule, no matter how you staff the project, are virtually nil. And if you're going to finish late anyway, you'd better consider now whether it will look better or worse for you not to have added the extra staff that upper management is willing to furnish early in the project. Even if that early staff allocation turns out to be

Figure 32-2   Hurried-up project (aborted staffing).

Figure 32-3   Early overstaffing to accommodate a deadline.

wasted, your political situation may be safer with all those people on-board early than if you were to proceed leanly staffed through the first six months. Such early understaffing—as it's sure to be viewed by disappointed upper management—may make you look like a Little Leaguer.

How common is it that projects are overstaffed early for such political reasons? Oh, not very. Probably no more than 90 percent of all projects suffer from early overstaffing.

It is a sad comment on the prevailing culture in development organizations that, in spite of all the talk about "lean and mean," it is politically unsafe for a manager to run a project leanly staffed through the key analysis and design activities.

Fragmentation Again

When people's time is wasted in unnecessary meetings or by early overstaffing, they'll know it. They'll be frustrated and they'll know why. If there is enough of such waste, they'll probably let *you* know about it, too. So these problems, though serious, are at least not invisible. There is, however, one way that people's time gets wasted that is likely to go unnoticed, and thus uncorrected. This has to do with the time fragmentation we first mentioned in Chapter 23, "Teamicide." The point there was that fragmenting any knowledge worker's time over many different tasks assures that he or she will be thrust into two or more different work groups, none of which is likely to jell into a real team.

Fragmented time is almost certain to be teamicidal, but it also has another insidious effect: It is guaranteed to waste the individual's time. A worker with multiple assignments—a little new development, some maintenance of a legacy product, some sales support, and perhaps a bit of end user hand-holding—will spend a significant part of each day switching gears. This time is largely invisible. The worker sets aside a design task to field a telephone call, works with the caller for twenty minutes to offer guidance about reconfiguring a database on one of the company's early products, and then turns back to the design task. If you were standing beside this person with a stopwatch, you would probably have noted no wasted time at all. The waste is concealed in the slow restart of his or her design work, the direct result of interrupted flow.

Fragmentation is particularly injurious when two of the tasks involve qualitatively different kinds of work habits. Thus, the mix of a design task (which requires lots of immersion time, relative quiet, and quality interaction time with a small group) with a telephone support task (which requires instant interruptibility, constant availability, quick change of focus) is sure to make progress on the more think-intensive of these tasks virtually impossible. The time wasted continually trying to get restarted is perceived only as frustration by the worker. You may never hear about it, because the people who suffer from this problem are all too likely to blame themselves.

Respecting Your Investment

My consulting over these last few decades has, for some reason, required more and more travel to Europe. I have begun taking the day flights from Boston to London, as they seem to be less of a trial for my now permanently jet-lagged body. Unfortunately, most of the other European capitals are served only by night flights out of Boston. I railed against this until an airline employee patiently pointed out to me that his company was reluctant to let a giant investment like a 747 sit on the tarmac for all the extra hours that would be required to connect an east-west day flight with a west-east day flight. 747s, after all, represent a ton of money.

—TDM

The human capital invested in your workforce also represents a ton of money. If your company employs a few thousand knowledge workers, it could easily have enough invested in them to be the equivalent of a modern wide-body aircraft. Wasting the time of that huge investment is money poured down the drain.

33

E(vil) Mail

Yes, your e-mail In-box is full. Very impressive. But what is it full of?

In Days of Yore

Before e-mail, we coordinated distant people by letter. A letter used to cost a hundred dollars or more in today's money, to dictate, transcribe, type, correct, retype, and post. It would take three days to a week to deliver. Another hundred dollars of effort on the other end to reply and another three days to a week to send it back. Today, we effect the same two-way communication at a hundredth of the cost and a thousandth of the time. But are we better off for it? Did we pocket the savings, or did we plow them back into hundreds of times more coordination?

You know the answer to that. We're coordinating an order of magnitude more than we ever did before.

I had a Canadian client named Diane who let drop that she had a two-hour commute in each direction between home and work. I commiserated, but she said it was no big deal. "This is Canada," she said, "so we have great wireless service all along the rail routes. And I have a BlackBerry. So I do my e-mail on the way to work and on the way home."

—TDM

Great. That's four hours a day of e-mail. And that's if she never looks at her e-mail at all during work hours. But you know she does.

We've become so used to tons of coordinating e-mail that we now take it for granted. Time to ask the key question: Can this be good?

A family therapist will tell you that when one person in a relationship over-functions, the others are sure to under-function. When one sibling leaps up to clear the table and wash the dishes, you're liable to see the others slipping off to do something more amusing. Could that be happening in your organization? When you over-coordinate the people who work for you, they're all too likely to under-coordinate their own efforts. But self-coordination and mutual coordination among peers is the hallmark of graceful teamwork. Watch a decent fast break in basketball or in hockey, and now imagine how it would work if every pass could only happen if and when the coach gave the signal from the sideline.

A decent coach understands that his or her job is not to coordinate interaction, but to help people learn to self-coordinate. We think that's the job of a knowledge-work manager as well. If you buy that idea, most coordinating e-mail is part of the problem, not part of the solution.

Corporate Spam

After decades of assault by malicious spammers, most organizations have pretty much figured out how to filter out the dregs and make sure that their people are only receiving non-spam e-mail from the outside. That's a great tribute to the valiant efforts of your network support group. But they haven't really solved the spam problem because most of the spam in your In-box comes from co-workers. Of course, you're not used to thinking of such messages as spam, but most of them are. Any message that is sent to one person with copies to half a dozen or more other recipients is candidate spam. The person it was directed to probably needed to see it, but how about the others? Were you on the receiving end because some action was required of you, or were you just included FYI?

An easy test for corporate spam is to apply some secure-organization thinking. When security is key, information is routed on a need-to-know basis. Imagine going through today's e-mail onslaught, asking about each and every arriving message, "Do I need to know this?" How many messages would pass the test? The ones that don't are a kind of internal taxation, using up your time and the time of others. No wonder so many of us are forever wondering why we go through whole days without actually getting any work done.

What Does "FYI" Even Mean?

The e-mail message that you dutifully read through that didn't pass the need-to-know test was presumably intended For Your Information. But if you didn't need to know it, of what value is the information?

What was going on in the mind of the person who added you to the CC line? There are lots of possibilities, most of them less than totally admirable:

- "If I don't send this around, how will anyone know I'm working?"
- "I don't dare *not* send this because people will complain if anything happens that they don't know about."
- "This is an open organization, so everybody has to see everything."
- "I want this widely seen because it shows what a great writer I am."

All of these are signs of organizational dysfunction. If people don't dare send anything out without copying *you,* that may be a sign of personal dysfunction. What tacit message are you sending them that makes them send every single message to you?

Is This an Open Organization or a Commune?

The phrase "open organization" has a warm touchy-feely sound to it. It suggests that people are proud of their work and happy to have it seen by others. We all want to work with people like that. But let's be reasonable about it: It's nice if people allow you to *pull* information from them about what they're doing, but less nice if they *push* it on you. Less nice still if what they seem to want to push onto you is everything. Our view is,

> Life is short. If you need to know everything in order to do anything, you're not going to get much done.

Repeal Passive Consent

One of the reasons that organizations are bogged down with everybody plowing through endless numbers of endless e-mails is that there is an unwritten rule at work. The rule is,

> Silence gives consent.

If someone sends you an e-mail that proposes to do some wacky thing and you don't object, under this rule you have effectively given your consent. If you find yourself spending hours each day reading through stuff that is of no real value to you, chances are it is because you have to worry about your consent being taken for granted because your name was on the CC line.

To free yourself and everyone else of this drudgery, you need to repeal the rule. Without knowing the ins and outs of your organization, we can't say how you need to go about it. But it's worth doing. An effective repeal—establishing that only explicit consent gives consent—could save your organization person-centuries of wasted time.

Building a Spam-less Self-Coordinating Organization

You may not be able to transform your whole company, but you can make important change in the work modes of people who work with you and under you. Start by stating in explicit terms that corporate spam is unwelcome. One of our clients even built an e-mail filter that rejected—with a polite advisory—e-mail that had his address only in the CC line or that had too many total recipients. He was at the top of the hierarchy, so he didn't have to worry about inadvertently insulting anyone above him. The lesson was quickly apparent to everyone who worked for him. They not only stopped sending him corporate spam but stopped sending it to each other as well.

Do the need-to-know test on your incoming e-mail, but do it, too, on the messages you send out. Each time you're inclined to send a coordinating e-mail to a colleague or to anyone who works for you, think about what steps you have to make to coach that person to self-coordinate. Don't expect this to be easy. Telling someone what to do *is* easy, while instilling self-coordinating abilities in that same person is much more complicated. But it pays off in the long run. If you need to puzzle long and hard over how to make it happen, remember that's why you make the big bucks.

34

Making Change Possible

"People hate change . . .
and that's because people hate change. . . .
I want to be sure that you get my point.
People *really* hate change. They *really, really* do."
—*Steve McMenamin*
Principal, The Atlantic Systems Guild

S teve made this statement to an audience of IT managers who were attending the Guild's 1996 London Conference. More than a little troubled by this view, at first the managers were pretty comfortable with rejecting it: "Hey, we build systems that change how people work and play. We try hard to make sure that the changes will be for the better. We explain how the new way will be better; sometimes, we even use precise geometric logic. Why would any rational person resist any change for the better?" To the protesters, Steve retorted, "You don't get it. I'm sorry, but people really, truly hate change. That's the problem: They're not rejecting a particular change on its merits; they're rejecting *any* change. And that's because people hate change." The examples he offered were devastating. Little by little, the message got through, and the crisis counselors had to be called in.

We need to talk about change because it is our business. More than being just system builders, we are change agents. Every time we deliver a new system, we are obliging people to change the way they do their work; we might be redefining their jobs entirely. We are demanding that they change, and while we're at it, our own organizations are demanding that we change, too. The emerging technologies and the building cycle-time pressures are forcing us to change how we build our products.

And Now, a Few Words from Another Famous Consultant

And it should be considered that nothing is more difficult to handle, more doubtful of success, nor more dangerous to manage, than

203

to put oneself at the head of introducing new orders. For the in-
troducer has all those who benefit from the old orders as enemies,
and he has lukewarm defenders in all those who might benefit
from the new orders.

—*Niccolò Machiavelli (1513)*[1]

We tend to think of Machiavelli as a cynic, but he almost certainly fancied himself a realist. He didn't set out to cast mankind in the most unflattering light, only to state the bald truth as he saw it. He wrote *The Prince* as a primer for the young Lorenzo de' Medici, who was ascending to govern the city-state of Florence. (The de' Medici family built an enclosed elevated walkway over the Arno, connecting their castle with the government building, to minimize the chances for assassination. Look for the walkway when you visit Florence; it's still there.) The book's purpose was to acquaint the young prince with reality, however pleasant or un-.

"For the introducer has all those who benefit from the old orders as enemies, and he has lukewarm defenders in all those who might benefit from the new orders." Notice the equation is unbalanced against change. While you risk making enemies of those who have mastered the old ways—you are forcing them back to the uncomfortable position of novice—you receive only minor support from those who would gain. Why is that? Why are those who stand most to gain from the change still half-hearted in their support? That's because people hate change. When we start out to change, it is never certain that we will succeed. And the uncertainty is more compelling than the potential for gain.

In years past, I served as Chair of the National Software Methods Conference, held each spring in Florida. The first year, I made some opening remarks and handed out a questionnaire for all the participants to complete. I asked all sorts of questions about what methods and tools they used to build software. One question I asked was, "What method or tool has been seriously introduced in your organization but has failed to become common practice?" I collected the responses, to report the results back to the attendees by the close of the conference. I started making a list of failed methods and tools, but stopped when I noticed something much simpler and clearer: Everything had failed, at least somewhere. The real irony is that when I did report back, I took the list of failures and asked if anybody was using those methods or tools regularly. I got a positive response on every single one. Everything works, and everything fails. What is going on here?

—TRL

---

1. N. Machiavelli, *The Prince*, trans. H. C. Mansfield, Jr. (Chicago: University of Chicago Press, 1985), p. 23.

That's a Swell Idea, Boss. I'll Get Right on It.

Whenever you attempt to instigate a change, you can expect a variety of responses. Jerry Johnson, one-time director of the Menninger Foundation, has proposed that there is a pattern to this variety, something he calls the "Resistance-to-Change Continuum." It looks like Figure 34–1.

Everyone falls someplace on the continuum in the way he or she will respond to a change.

Looking at the continuum, ask yourself, "Who of these are my potential enemies, and who are my possible supporters?" Clearly, the Militantly Opposed are dangerous; they will seek to return to the old status quo at any cost. You might conclude that the Blindly Loyal are good guys and the others are whiners, that the Blindly Loyal are allies and the other groups are enemies.

Johnson pointed out that this view is all wrong. For example, we need to be aware of the danger posed by the Blindly Loyal. They are probably fairly powerless, and they will jump onto whatever appears hot. They follow *le fad du jour:* "We gotta stop the accounting package installation right now because we can do it better ourselves with an intranet-based system using Java Decaf. Wait. Hold the Decaf. I just saw an ad on the *Computing This Nanosecond* Web site for Double-Java Latte with foamy applets." They will withdraw their support as quickly as they give it in order to hop on some new bandwagon.

Johnson asserts that the Believers But Questioners are the only meaningful potential allies of any change. The two extremes, Blindly Loyal and Militantly Opposed, are the real enemies. The success of your change will depend on how you manage the Believers But Questioners. Don't count on logic, by the way, as your trump card: These on-the-fence, maybe-baby allies are never going to be swayed solely by a rational discussion of why the proposed new way will be so much better than the current situation. Here is something to repeat to yourself whenever you set out to ask people to change:

> *MANTRA: The fundamental response to change is not logical, but emotional.*

1. Blindly Loyal (Ask no questions.)
2. Believers but Questioners
   a. Skeptics ("Show me.")
   b. Passive Observers ("What's in it for me?")
   c. Opposed (Fear of Change)
   d. Opposed (Fear of Loss of Power)
3. Militantly Opposed (Will Undermine and Destroy)

increasing
resistance

Figure 34–1   Resistance-to-Change Continuum.

As systems developers, we have selected ourselves into the world of cool, calming, rational thought. Either our code compiles, or it doesn't. The compiler is never happy for us, nor mad at us. Perhaps this is why we tend to apply logic as our main device for resolving disputes.

You may catch yourself patiently explaining to your kid: "I know you want a bike, but it is neither your birthday nor is it Christmas, the cultural dates upon which gifts may reasonably be expected. If you have accumulated sufficient allowance, you may proceed with the purchase yourself." And you may be frustrated by a not-very-logical response like, "But I want a bike! I want it right now."

When we argue logically for change, one tactic is to contrast how the new world will be (good) compared to the current situation (bad). But think: Who helped implement the current situation? Who are the masters of the ways that we currently work? Could these people possibly take offense at any diminution of the current mode? Damn right they could. William Bridges, in *Managing Transitions*, suggests that we never demean our old ways. Instead, we need to *celebrate* the old as a way to help change happen. For example,

> Folks, the CGS Close-in Guidance System has been running for 14 years. We estimate that it has perfectly handled over 1,000,000 take-offs and landings. The hardware platform has become technically obsolete, and there is some new remote sensing technology that we can take advantage of. Now we have the chance to redesign and rebuild the entire system. We need you and your expertise gained over these years of successful CGS experience to help us succeed in this effort.

It's worth keeping in mind that *any* improvement involves change.

You can never improve if you can't change at all.

—TDM

A Better Model of Change

The way most of us tend to think about change is depicted in Figure 34–2.

In this (naïve) view, an idea, a simple vision of "a better way" to do things, effects a direct change from the old to the new. "We were perking along in the old mode when Harvey had a sudden inspiration, and we switched over to a new and altogether superior way of doing business." Honestly, it can't be that simple. It isn't. Contrast that naïve model of change with the way an expert in family therapy, the late Virginia Satir, looked at change (Figure 34–3).

Figure 34-2 Naïve model of how change happens.

Figure 34-3 Satir Change Model.

Change involves at least the four stages shown in Figure 34-3, never fewer. There is no chance of effecting meaningful change without going through the two intermediate stages.

According to Satir's model, change happens upon the introduction of a foreign element: a catalyst for change. Without a catalyst, there is no recognition of the desirability of change. The foreign element can be an outside force or it can be the recognition that your world has somehow changed.

> **Outside force:** A measurement consultant walks into your office and announces that your company is performing in the lower quartile of all companies in your industry. Hmmmm.
>
> OR
>
> **The world changes:** The quarterly sales of your flagship product drop for the very first time in its history. Owww.

When you try to institute change, the first thing you hit is Chaos. You've been there before. It's when you are convinced that you are worse off than before with this new tool, new procedure, or new technique. People are saying things like, "If we just jettison this new stuff, maybe we'll get back on schedule. . . ." You are suffering from the dip in the learning curve, and the assessment that the change is the problem may well be right, at least for the moment. You *are* worse off, for now. This is part of the reason why response to change is so emotional. It is frustrating and embarrassing to abandon approaches and methods you have long since mastered, only to become a novice again. Nobody enjoys that sense of floundering; you just know you would be better off with the old way. Unfortunately, this passage through Chaos is absolutely necessary, and it can't be shortcut.

The transforming idea is something that people in Chaos can grab onto as offering hope that the end of the suffering is near. A structured huddle is sometimes the best medicine: "I think that we're getting the hang of E-SOA authentication, but how about a daily meeting at four o'clock for all of us to go over our class definitions together?"

The Practice-and-Integration phase occurs on the upswing of the learning curve. You are not yet completely comfortable as you are not yet proficient at the new, but you perceive that the new is now beginning to pay off or at least to show promise.

You have reached the New Status Quo when what you changed to becomes what you do. An interesting characteristic of human emotion is that the more painful the Chaos, the greater the perceived value of the New Status Quo—if you can get there.

The reason the Satir model is so important is that it alerts us that Chaos is an integral part of change. With the more naïve two-stage model, we don't expect Chaos. When it occurs, we mistake it for the New Status Quo. And since the New Status Quo seems so chaotic, we think, "Whoops, looks like we blew it; let's change back." The change-back message is bound to be heard loud and clear in the middle of any ambitious change. When you're looking for it, your chances of dealing sensibly with it are much improved.

Safety First

Change won't even get started unless people feel safe—and people feel safe when they know they will not be demeaned or degraded for proposing a change, or trying to get through one. Temporary loss of mastery is embarrassing enough for most of us; catching any kind of gratuitous flack for floundering in Chaos guarantees that everyone will flee back to the security of the Old Status Quo.

Our natural fear of Chaos may help to explain why learning something as a child appears so much easier than learning the same thing as an adult.

Watching and listening to adults and children on their first ski trips, we get the distinct impression that adults are not so much concerned with injuring themselves as they are with making fools of themselves. Kids almost never have that thought. They may actually choose to fall down in the snow, to roll in it, to throw it, to eat it. (Our natural adult response to snow is to shovel it so we won't slip.) On the slopes, adults don't want to fall where they can be seen by those in the chairlift. The anticipated humiliation is enough to keep them in the lodge. But give a healthy kid a lesson or two with a ski instructor, and it's, "Look at me, I'm Picabo Street!"

—Tim and Tom, Amateur Behaviorists

How many times have you heard that some new technique is going to be used because it is the only chance to make the hard-and-fast deadline, and that if the deadline is missed, there will be hell to pay? The setup of the change has already made its outcome more than a little dubious. The kid-like willingness to throw ourselves into a potentially embarrassing endeavor is defeated by the potential for ridicule.

Paradoxically, change only has a chance of succeeding if failure—at least a little bit of failure—is also okay.

35

Organizational Learning

S ome organizations can learn and some can't. Some can learn a lesson in the abstract but can't change themselves to take advantage of what they have learned. Some can learn, but the pace of their learning is offset by the pace of their unlearning. We all understand that the difference between being among the learning washed, as opposed to among the learning unwashed, is a matter of vital importance, because non-learners cannot expect to prosper for very long without learning, a critical improvement mechanism.

Experience and Learning

The first thing to realize about organizational learning is that it is not the same as simple accumulation of experience. By the 1930s, for example, the French army had accumulated hundreds of years of experience in guarding the eastern borders, but it still proposed the Maginot Line as a way to hold back the Germans. That decision and the events of May 1940 proved to the world that the French had not learned a key lesson about the shifting balance between armor and mobility.

Similarly, high-tech organizations may accumulate experience at an astonishing rate, but there is no guarantee that their learning will keep track.

One of my clients had a long history of software development, going back more than forty years. Through much of this period, it kept a thousand or more software developers at work. So, its managers could brag, without exaggeration, that they had more than forty thousand person-years of software experience. I was

continues

211

continued

greatly impressed: Imagine all that learning being brought to bear on each new project. So I asked a group of them, "When you send a new manager off to run a new software project, what words of wisdom do you whisper in his or her ear?" They thought for just a moment and then gave their answer, almost in unison: "Good luck."

—TRL

Experience gets turned into learning when an organization alters itself to take account of what experience has shown. This alteration takes two forms, which are different enough to talk about separately:

> *The organization instills new skills and approaches in its people.*

OR

> *The organization redesigns itself to operate in some different manner.*

In the first case, the change is the direct result of added human capital (see Chapter 20 for more on this). If the retrained people leave, the investment is lost and the learning is gone. In the second case, the change is temporarily in the heads of individuals who implement the redesign. Eventually, it becomes part of the bone-knowledge of the organization, but in the interim it resides only in the participants' minds. In this case, loss of key people during the transition can jeopardize the learning.

In either case, the self-transforming organization has to face up to the following irreducible risk:

> *Learning is limited by an organization's ability to keep its people.*

When turnover is high, learning is unlikely to stick or can't take place at all. In such an organization, attempts to change skills or to introduce redesigned procedures are an exercise in futility. They may even act perversely to accelerate the rate of employee turnover.

A Redesign Example

Some of the most compelling stories of organizational learning involve redesign of the supplier chain. This requires a confident hand at the helm and a willingness to think outside of organizational boundaries. Consider the following example, elaborating on a suggestion first made by Nicholas Negroponte at The Camden Conference on Telecommunications some years ago:

> *A company like Amazon.com has an integral (and potentially exploitable) link to whatever corporate partner it chooses for delivery of its products to the end consumer. In its current form, the company may have Federal Express pick up books from one of its warehouses, and fly them to Memphis (FedEx's hub city) and then on to the airport nearest to the consumer. Now suppose that Amazon were to locate a warehouse in the field beside the FedEx Memphis airstrip. The sale of each book could still be processed at Amazon's Seattle headquarters, but now the pick list and shipping information could be transmitted digitally to the Memphis warehouse, where the orders would be assembled. Advantage to Amazon: reduction by half of the shipping distance for each order.*[1]

Organizations that can make this kind of change can do it again and again. You might wonder what it is that allows them to be so agile.

The Key Question About Organizational Learning

The key question about organizational learning is not *how* it is done but *where*. When an organization changes itself as much as Amazon has over the years, there has to be a small but active learning center that conceives of, designs, and directs the change. (This kind of ambitious change can't be invented by a committee or by the organization as a whole.) The locus of early change activity—the learning—has to be located somewhere on the organization chart. Where?

It's tempting to say that it happens at the top. But tops of organizations, in our experience, are not so much focused on day-to-day operations. Presidents of large- to medium-size companies, for example, may spend most of their time making acquisitions (or fighting them off).

There is a nice, egalitarian ring to the notion that the learning center might be at the bottom. But don't count on this happening in the real world. People at the bottom are typically too constrained by the organizational boundaries, and might be blind to important possibilities. In any event, they rarely have the power to effect change.

---

1. Remarks made at the Pop!Tech Conference in Camden, Maine, October, 1997.

If the key learning doesn't happen at the top and it doesn't happen at the bottom, then it has to occur somewhere in the middle. That means the most natural learning center for most organizations is at the level of that much-maligned institution, middle management. This squares exactly with our own observation that successful learning organizations are always characterized by strong middle management.

It's worth pointing out that downsizings, when they happen, are almost always targeted at middle management. In other words, the proverbial "tightening ship" activity that has its vogue every few years is often at the expense of organizational learning. After such an exercise, an organization's learning center may be destroyed.

The Management Team

Flattening the org. chart by gutting middle management is a sure recipe for decreased learning. But the converse is not necessarily true: Holding on to middle management doesn't, by itself, make learning more likely to prosper. There is another ingredient required for that, one that is seldom evaluated properly and almost never cultivated. In order for a vital learning center to form, middle managers must communicate with each other and learn to work together in effective harmony. This is an extremely rare phenomenon.

Almost all companies have something they call the Management Team, typically made up of middle-management peers. As we observed earlier, applying the word *team* to a group doesn't assure that it will have any of the characteristics of a team. It may still be a poorly knit collection of individuals who have no common goals, common values, or blended skills. This is usually the case with most so-called management teams.

A good helping of the teamicidal effects we noted in Chapters 23 and 24 ("Teamicide" and "Teamicide Revisited") is at work on "teams" of managers: Group members are made defensive, burdened by bureaucracy, assigned fragmented tasks, physically separated, pressured to work overtime, and goaded into competition with each other. With all that going against them, they are unlikely to merge into a meaningful whole.

To make matters worse, they don't have the one thing that any team needs in order to jell: common ownership of the work product. Anything that gets accomplished in such a group is likely to be the accomplishment of one of its members, not the group as a whole. The more competitive the managers are, the more pronounced this effect. We have even encountered extreme cases in which the rule was: "If something looks good, grab it; if you can't grab it, kill it."

The Management Team is, most often, a sad misnomer, a mockery of the kind of behavior and attitude that characterizes a healthy team. The members sit together regularly at status meetings, taking turns talking to the upper manager. But they have little to do with each other.

Danger in the White Space

The most likely learning center for any sizable organization is the white space that lies between and among middle managers. If this white space becomes a vital channel of communication, if middle managers can act together as the redesigners of the organization, sharing a common stake in the result, then the benefits of learning are likely to be realized. If, on the other hand, the white space is empty of communication and common purpose, learning comes to a standstill. Organizations in which middle managers are isolated, embattled, and fearful are nonstarters in this respect.

36

The Making of Community

In this chapter, we turn to what great managers do best: the making of community. A need for community is something that is built right into the human firmware.

During my school years, my family insisted on moving almost every year, and I rarely finished a school year in the same town where I had begun it. I had a complete change of friends, acquaintances, and teachers nearly every year. One of the few constants in my life was the set of basal readers that were used by the New England schools in those years; these books were used in every school that I attended. The text concerned a family that had lived in one town, a place called Winchester, since the 1770s. Each year, the class studied a subsequent generation of the family, until by sixth grade we had followed it through the Revolution and all the way into the early twentieth century. While the characters in that family are long since forgotten to me, I retain a vivid memory of the town. Winchester was a place where everyone knew everyone, where people stayed put from generation to generation, where a lost dog or a troubled child was everybody's concern, and where you looked out for your neighbors when calamity happened. If I have any roots at all, I guess they're in Winchester.

—TDM

If there is something deep inside you that responds to the idea of such a town, it's probably because you don't presently live in one. The lovely little Winchesters of the world began to change and disappear in the 1920s. Most of us today live in places that aren't really communities at all. People don't know their neighbors very well, they commute out to work someplace else, and nobody expects the kids to settle down in the same town. Bedroom communities, in particular, are all bedroom and no community.

But we still have a strong need for community. The complicated truth of our times is that most of our towns no longer satisfy this need. It is instead in the workplace that we have our best chance of finding community. If it's there to be found . . .

Digression on Corporate Politics

Community doesn't just happen on the job. It has to be made. The people who make it are the unsung heroes of our work experience.

The science of making communities, making them healthy and satisfying for all, is called politics. We hasten to add that it's not the shameless shenanigans of corporate infighting that we're going to address here; those are the pathologies of politics. What we need to look at instead is "Politics, the Noble Science," as first described by Aristotle.

Aristotle included Politics among the five interlinked Noble Sciences that together make up Philosophy. The five are,

- **Metaphysics:** the study of existence, the nature of the universe and all its contents

- **Logic:** the ways we may know something, the set of permissible conclusions we may draw based on our perceptions, and some sensible rules of deduction and inference

- **Ethics:** what we know about man and what we may deduce and infer (through Logic) about acceptable interactions between pairs of individuals

- **Politics:** how we may logically extend Ethics to the larger group, the science of creating and managing such groups consistent with ethical behavior and logical recognition of the metaphysical entities—*humans* and the *community* made up of humans

- **Aesthetics:** the appreciation of symbols and images of metaphysical reality, which are pleasing to the extent that they are logically consistent and that they inform us about ethical interaction and/or political harmony

You may be quite sure that you want no part of office politics of the sleazy kind, but Aristotelian Politics is something else entirely. Aristotelian Politics

is the key practice of good management. Refusing to be political in the Aristotelian sense is disastrous; it is an abnegation of the manager's real responsibility. Similarly, senior workers at all levels share some responsibility for
community-building. They are the elders of whatever community does form.

Why It Matters

An organization that succeeds in building a satisfying community tends to
keep its people. When the sense of community is strong enough, no one
wants to leave. The investment made in human capital is thus retained, and
upper management finds itself willing to invest more. When the company
invests more in its people, the people perform better and feel better about
themselves and about their company. This makes them still less likely to move
on. The positive reinforcement here is all to the good.

Of course, even the best sense of on-the-job community doesn't assure
that you will keep all your people forever. Some will know they have to leave
to advance their own careers or for whatever other reason. However, when
people do leave such an organization, they tend to time their departures to
minimally inconvenience the community. This is an extraordinary boon to
anyone doing project work, since it means that workers are unlikely to leave
during the project. This effect alone, of departing only at project end, is worth
more than all the process improvement your organization is likely to make
over the next decade.

So far, we've discussed only the tangible, dollars-and-cents benefits. There
is an intangible at work here, too, one that's liable to have even more significance to you than all the rest. To consider it, cast your mind forward, just for a
moment, to that day in the distant future, when you are about to cash in your
chips. You're on your deathbed at the grand old age of, let's say, a hundred
and one. You're in no great discomfort, only old. At this age, your thoughts
are all in the past. You're taking stock. You ask yourself the question, What
really mattered in my life and what didn't? It's no great surprise that many
of the concerns that utterly obsessed you all those years ago (for example,
getting that humongous version 27 build of WhizBang v6.1.1 to stabilize)
don't figure very prominently in your deathbed assessment. No, you're much
more likely to think about warm family relations, kids and grandkids, the
house and all its memories. Any contribution from your work? Well, sure, it
was nice to be part of the coming-of-age of the Information Era. It was good
to rise to the top of a company, or nearly to the top, to have your chance at
setting directions. That was nice. But don't forget that you also succeeded at
creating a real community within that company, something that people loved

and respected and gave their allegiance to. Now, that was an accomplishment. That's got to figure very prominently in your sense of what you have done with your life. The pleasure you take from that—like the pleasure that Michelangelo must have felt, mulling over his contributions—need have no very strong connection to their cash value at the time. This was a creation. This was Art, you tell yourself, and the person who made it happen was an Artist.

Pulling Off the Magic

Okay, so community is good, so it is an admirable goal to build community in the workplace. How is it done?

We are not going to presume to set forth a formula for such a complicated matter. There is no formula. Like any work of art, your success at fostering community is going to require substantial talent, courage, and creativity. It will also need an enormous investment of time. The work will not be completed by you alone; at best, you will be the catalyst. The form of your creation will not be very much like anyone else's.

So, in place of a formula, we offer instead an example, a single example. The example comes from one of our client companies, a company where one enterprising manager stepped in and changed the culture forever. This catalytic genius persuaded the organization to build itself around a school. The school is made up of a day-care and preschool center, plus classes for kindergarteners through fifth graders. The school is for the children of employees.

No doubt you can see the dollars-and-cents rationale for this, the unique advantage the company gained for hiring programmers and engineers in a tight market. But you'd have to walk through the company to see what the school does for community. You'd have to be there for that moment every afternoon when the teachers lead the entire student body through the whole facility. They make up a noisy, funny, triumphantly silly parade of little kids whooping it up and saying hello to everyone. You can hear them coming a mile away. All work pauses for the procession. There are lots of hugs. When it's over, everyone feels great.

Imagine having been the person responsible for that. Imagine having that to look back at from the age of a hundred and one.

PART V I

It's Supposed to Be Fun to Work Here

Somewhere deep in our ancestral memory is buried the notion that work is supposed to be onerous. If you enjoy doing something, it isn't really work. If you enjoy it enough, it's probably sinful. You ought not to do it too much or even at all. You certainly shouldn't be paid for it. What you really ought to do is find something else to work at, something that feels like work. Then you can be bored, tired, and generally miserable like everybody else.

If you're a manager, this vestigial memory requires you to make sure that your people never have any fun on the job. Any evidence of pleasure or joy in the workplace is a sure sign that some manager is not doing the job properly. Work is not being extracted with maximum efficiency from the workers; otherwise, they wouldn't be having such a good time.

Of course, nobody ever says outright that work ought not to be fun, but the idea is there, burned into our cultural subconsciousness. It turns up in the guilty sheepishness we feel if we're ever caught giggling in delight at the task at hand. It surfaces in our reluctant acceptance of the dress code, the anti-popcorn code, and the general furrowed-brow attitude that distinguishes so-called professionals from people who are enjoying themselves.

In Part VI, we'll address the opposite premise, that work should be fun.

37
Chaos and Order

There is something about human nature that makes us the implacable enemies of chaos. Whenever we encounter chaos, we roll up our sleeves and go right to work to replace it with order. Man-made order is everywhere . . . in the home, in the garden, in the way we comb our hair or organize our streets into neat grids. But it does not follow from this that we'd be happier if there were no more chaos. On the contrary, we'd be bored to tears. What chaos is left in modern society is a precious commodity. We have to be careful to conserve it and keep the greedy few from hogging more than their share.

We managers tend to be the greedy few. We often see chaos as our particular domain. We assume that it's our job to clean it up, all of it. The Open Kimono manager has a different approach. He or she is willing to leave small packets of chaos to others. The manager's job in this approach is to break it up and parcel it out. The people down below get to have the real fun of putting things shipshape.

Progress Is Our Most Important Problem

The amount of chaos is ever declining. This is particularly evident in new technological fields. Those people who were attracted to such areas years ago by the newness, the lack of order, feel a nostalgic fondness for the days when everything wasn't so awfully mechanical. Every great advance of the past thirty years has had the effect of reducing the craziness of our work. Of course, those advances were wonderful—we'd never want to go back to the old days—but still . . .

223

We're all eager to improve our methods and make the business of development a more orderly enterprise. That's progress. True, some of the crazy fun is lost in the process, but one person's fun may be another's agony (that project you thought was such a lark probably gave your boss an ulcer). In any event, progress toward more orderly, controllable methods is an unstoppable trend. The thoughtful manager doesn't want to stop the trend, but may nonetheless feel a need to replace some of the lost disorder that has breathed so much energy into the work. This leads to a policy of *constructive reintroduction of small amounts of disorder.*

Once the idea is stated so baldly, it's simple enough to compile a list of ways to implement this policy:

- Pilot projects
- War games
- Brainstorming
- Provocative training experiences
- Training, trips, conferences, celebrations, and retreats

For this list, we've limited ourselves to disorder-reintroduction techniques that we have seen used successfully. Your own list ought not to be so limited. A short brainstorming session on the subject (more about brainstorming below) will produce wild and wonderful possibilities.

Pilot Projects

A pilot project is one in which you set the fat book of standards aside and try some new and unproved technique. The new technique will be unfamiliar initially, and so you can expect to be inefficient at the start in applying it. This is a cost of change. On the other side of the ledger is the improvement in productivity gained from using the new technique. Also on the plus side of the ledger is the Hawthorne Effect, the boost in energy and interest that infuses your people when they're doing something new and different.

Are these two pluses likely to outweigh the minus caused by the learning curve? We'd be foolhardy to suggest that they always would. The nature of the change introduced matters a lot, as do the length of the project, the capability of the staff members, and the extent to which people believe in the technique they're trying out. Our experience is that pilot projects, projects that try out any modified approach, tend toward higher-than-average net productivity. That means you're likely to spend less money on a given project if you choose to run it as a pilot project with some new technique.

Should all projects therefore be pilot projects? Your organization would be in good company if it adopted that policy, sharing it with Fujitsu, parts of the Southern Company, and some divisions of IBM. In any event, it makes far more sense to run all projects as pilots than to run no projects as pilots.

There are two likely objections to any expanded program of piloting new techniques:

- Won't we run out of things to try out?

- Won't we further complicate the downstream activities (product support, customer training, and so on) by delivering inconsistent products?

The first objection makes sense only in the abstract. Most organizations, after decades of having a policy of testing new ideas rarely if ever, need not worry too much about running out of things to try. They could begin by trying all the good ideas they ignored during the last decades of the twentieth century, then moving on to the early twenty-first. By the time they're through with all those, another decade will have passed and there will be plenty more to try out.

As to the problem of inconsistent products passed downstream, you may as well admit that this is true anyway in even the most standardized shop. What present-day standardization has achieved is a *documentary consistency* among products, but nothing approaching meaningful *functional consistency*. In other words, standardization has mainly homogenized the paperwork associated with the products, rather than the products themselves. If the paper trail left by the project were a little different from standard, the added inconvenience would be small.

One caveat about pilot projects: Don't experiment with more than one aspect of development technology on any given project. For all the talk about the importance of standards, it's surprising how often managers abandon all standards on the rare project that is designated a pilot. They often try out new hardware, new software, new quality control procedures, matrix management, and new prototyping techniques, all on the same project.

A sensible approach to pilot projects is that they each be allowed to tinker with one component of the process. In the healthiest environment, project personnel would understand that they are encouraged to experiment with some single new technique on each project, but nonetheless expected to respect standards in other areas.

War Games

From our years of running the Coding War Games, we have learned that the sometimes raucous, competitive, no-lose experience can be a delightful source of constructive disorder. Our games are tailored for the software community, but the concept can be applied to virtually any field. Whatever your work, it can be an enjoyable experience to try your hand at a set of tailored problems, and to be able to compare your performance to a statistical performance profile of your peers. (Of course, the experience is only enjoyable as long as the security and confidentiality guarantees described in Chapter 8, "You Never Get Anything Done around Here between 9 and 5." are respected and you are thus assured that the game results won't be used against you.)

War games help you to evaluate your relative strengths and weaknesses and help the organization to observe its global strengths and weaknesses. For these reasons, two of our client companies began a program of annual war games, used by their employees to gauge improvements in their own skills over time. Once a year, they subjected themselves to the confidential testing process, much as you would submit yourself to a physical exam.

For the purpose of stimulating creative disorder, the most effective form of war game calls for participants to take part in teams. The following is one formula for such an exercise, a formula that we have tried out with some success (and enormous amusement):

- Select a small development project or well-defined task as a guinea pig. The best choice is an actual job from your organization, something that requires from one to two person-months of effort. Pick a problem that has some novelty and challenge, but that nonetheless makes broad use of your people's typical working skills.

- Conduct the project in a normal fashion up through publication of a concrete statement of work.

- Announce a 24-hour Project Tournament to be conducted on an upcoming weekend. Make sure everybody understands that you're not saving money at the expense of their weekend. Explain that the tournament is run over a weekend so the teams can have the place to themselves, not so you can save on manpower cost. Encourage people to form teams of four each and compete on a totally voluntary basis.

- Distribute the statement of work in advance, along with a statement of rules and objectives.

- On the day of the Tournament, only participants are present. Supply everything they need (food, machines, cots, copiers, conference rooms, whatever). Have all of the teams undertake the same work in head-to-head competition with each other.

- Have facilitators available to enforce the ground rules, ready to head off fatal problems and to make lots of noise over every milestone attained.

- Look for opportunities to make everyone a winner in some sense (elapsed-time winners, robust-product winners, clever-solution winners). Make a big fuss over any and all accomplishments.

- Install the winning product, or perhaps several winning products in parallel. Keep careful track over time of product stability, number of defects, level of user acceptance, cost to change, and whatever other parameters affect project success. Report meaningful data back to the teams.

When you pull this off successfully, people will tell you they've had the most exciting and enjoyable experience of their entire careers; nothing less than that is your goal. Expect to achieve that goal, though it may take a few tries.

Some things to keep in mind about experiences like the Project Tournament: First, these affairs cost money. Don't go into them hoping to gull your staff into building something on a Saturday that you would otherwise have to pay real wages for. Expect to spend several times more on a Project Tournament than you would on a conventional running of the same project. Second, invest a lot of time in making the problem specification particularly solid, bringing your facilitators up to speed, and building in lots of milestones and checkpoints. Third, invest some effort to assure the project's scope is about the right size for the amount of time allocated (no one has any fun if all the teams are defeated or if the tournament is finished an hour after it begins). Finally, look for opportunities to spend money generously on meals (in one tournament, we ordered lovely picnic lunches catered by a New York City restaurant, had dinner delivered, and dragged everybody off to Chinatown for 2 A.M. snacks).

Running the project through a whole night, for some reason, adds to the fun. People love an excuse to get tired together, to push back sleep and let their peers see them with their hair down, unshaved, rumpled, and grumpy, with no makeup or pretense. And it makes them feel more closely bound to each other:

> *During the event, I noticed [one of the participants] catching a catnap on the rug in the reception area. I'd known her for years before that and always thought her a bit stiff. But from that point on, I felt differently about her. I felt differently about all of them. We'd been through it together.*
>
> *—from a Project Tournament postmortem*

Brainstorming

Brainstorming is a structured interactive session, specifically targeted on creative insight. Up to half a dozen people get together to focus on a relevant problem. The rules of the session and the ploys used by the person in charge help to make it an enjoyable and disorderly experience, and often a truly rewarding one.

There aren't many rules. Since you're trying to introduce chaos into the thought process, rules don't have much of a place. As facilitator, you want to impress on everyone to strive for quantity of ideas, not quality, and to keep the proceedings loose, even silly. Sometimes an apparently foolish idea, one that wouldn't even be mentioned in a more formal session, can turn out to be the prize. There is no evaluation of proposed ideas during the brainstorming. The evaluation phase comes later. Discourage negative comments, like "That's a dumb idea," since dumb ideas often lead others to think of smart ideas.

As facilitator, try these ploys to restart participants' thinking when the idea flow slows down:

- Analogy thinking (How does nature solve this or some similar problem?)

- Inversion (How might we achieve the opposite of our goal?)

- Immersion (How might you project yourself into the problem?)

Training, Trips, Conferences, Celebrations, and Retreats

Perhaps this is a sad comment on the dismal corporate workplace, but everybody relishes a chance to get out of the office. The chance that workers relish most is one combining travel with their peers and a one-of-a-kind experience. It might be going off together for a training session, particularly a provocative one, or taking in the International Conference On Whatever. All the better if the travel is to someplace exotic. You can send your people from Boston to a conference in London for about the same cost as sending them to a conference in St. Louis or Chula Vista.

Particularly when a team is forming, it makes good business sense to fight for travel money to get team members out of the office together. If there is a remote client site, ship them off all-expenses-paid to check out that territory. When there is a thought-intensive deliverable due, put them into a conference center or hotel. Give them the chance to fly together, eat out together, and work out their roles in the new team.

The Outward Bound schools make a thriving business of taking corporate groups into the wilderness and testing their mettle. Groups must make their way over Burma bridges and chutes, survive the waters of Penobscot Bay, or scale the face of Mount Katahdin. One day you're struggling with Supply Chain Management, and the next, you're hanging by your fingernails while a teammate belays you a line. Of course, the experience isn't cheap. By the time you count the cost of the school, travel, and lost days, it comes to at least several thousand dollars per person. In most companies, such an expense would be unthinkable. But what about the others, the ones who do invest in Outward Bound and the like? Are they missing something that is obvious to all the reasonable folks in the world? Or are they pushing the envelope to bring out the best in their people?

Is a few thousand dollars for a getaway experience too rich for your discretionary disorder budget? Maybe you could spring for a hundred dollars. One of the most innovative managers we've known had a penchant for putting on unexpected lunches for his staff. He once went down to the city street and hired a hot dog vendor—complete with cart, sauerkraut, yellow mustard, and a blue and orange umbrella—to take the elevator up thirty floors and serve lunch to the team. The lunch was a nutritionist's nightmare but a sociologist's dream come true. Those who were there got high on good spirits and began to do bits and skits about their work, their managers, and each other. The noise level went up with their enthusiasm. It cost maybe a hundred dollars and has been talked about ever since. Of course, that manager wrote it up as a business lunch, but it wasn't a lunch at all, it was a celebration.

There can be no question that good sense and order are desirable components of our workday. There's also a place for adventure, silliness, and small amounts of constructive disorder.

38

Free Electrons

In our grandparents' generation, work was usually structured rigidly within a corporate context: You worked for a company, and you punched a clock or kept regular hours. You received a paycheck, same this week as last. Those above you in the hierarchy were treated with respect and deference: "Of course, sir. I'll get cracking on that right away, sir." It didn't seem like a life's work you were embarked upon—it seemed more like a *job*. But things have changed.

One of my college roommates arranged a get-together of members of our graduating class. Of the twenty people who showed up that night, only one turned out to have a "job" in the normal sense of that word. All the others were self-employed or freelancing or contracting their services or working in some other nontraditional mode.

—TDM

The Cottage-Industry Phenomenon

It's hardly hot news these days that lots of our peers are working as cottage-industry entrepreneurs. They contract their time by the day, week, or even years for programming or design work or, sometimes, management. There are agencies that specialize in connecting these independents with organizations that need their talents.

Some of the most staid companies and institutions find themselves doing business with independents. They might prefer to hire their own people rather than deal with contractors and freelancers, but what can they do? It's always a seller's market for expert services. They end up doing business with dozens of little organizations with names like William Alonzo & Associates (there are no associates, just Bill) or the Fat City Smarts Company. Some of the folks they have to work with are positively flaky: They want to work when they want to work, perhaps doing one project and then taking off two or three months to go skiing. Erghhh! How unprofessional.

If you're a Captain of Industry, the cottage-industry phenomenon can be more than a little upsetting. Not only are the entrepreneurs inclined to be uppity, they are a terrible example to your employees. They've got more freedom, more time off, more choice of work. They're having more fun. They often make more money.

Fellows, Gurus, and Intrapreneurs

Organizations are under increasing pressure to offer attractive in-house alternatives to their best people lest they become part of the cottage-industry phenomenon. One such alternative is a position with loosely stated responsibilities so that the individual has a strong say in defining the work. The charter might read, "Investigate new methods for the twenty-first century," or "Put together a new and exciting training sequence," or "Design an ideal workstation complex for developers."

In extreme cases, the charter is a blank check; if your corporation is fortunate enough to have a self-motivated super-achiever on board, it's enough to say, "Define your own job." Our colleague Steve McMenamin characterizes these workers as "free electrons," since they have a strong role in choosing their own orbits.

The trend to create an increasing number of free electron positions is more than just a response to the threat of the cottage industry. The reason there are so many gurus and fellows and intrapreneurs and internal consultants in healthy modern companies is quite simply that companies profit from them. The people in these positions contribute disproportionately to the organizations that employ them. They are motivated to make the positions created for them pay off for their companies. Read what various of our colleagues had to say about consultancy jobs they held within healthy companies near the apex of their corporate careers:

Where I go and what I do are things pretty much defined by myself. Management recognized that the company needed someone looking into all the directions we weren't currently following, hence my unstructured charter. It puts me into the import business, constantly on the lookout for new ways the technology could help us. The position makes me more loyal to the company, but less loyal to my old profession of information science—a good idea is welcome wherever it comes from. I define my success based on the value it brings the company. It's almost as though the company were my own. There are lots of people who have, someplace in their closets, an intrapreneurial hat. You've just got to find out who they are and get them to wear it.

—Michael L. Mushet
Manager of Technology Research, Southern California Edison

I've had a number of different positions in my years with the company, but only one of them had existed before I came along. I've been able to define my position, to a large degree, ever since. There is always someone in an organization that's willing to sponsor meaningful work in a new area, at least up to a point. Where it works best, upper management has bought into a person, rather than into a concept. The person then defines and sells the concept. Everyone ought to have some responsibility for broad area goals, and some freedom to pursue them.

—Richard Branton
Manager, DAIS, Southern Company Services, Inc.

It works when people are self-motivated, and when they let reality dictate their directions to some extent. I'm constantly being dragged back into reality because the interests of the company dictate it. A lot of pure research is dead end. It's important to keep yourself focused on applied technology, because that can always be made useful to the organization. The whole idea of a loose charter can backfire, too, as it has at Xerox. Some of the best people there got to feel that the company was never going to use the good ideas they were coming up with [at PARC], and so they left."

—Bill Bonham
Fellow, MicroSage Computer Systems, Inc.

No Parental Guidance

In Soviet society, particularly among Communist Party members, there was a pervasive system of life counseling. Virtually every member was assigned a counselor, someone to meet with on a weekly basis to help make life decisions, to iron out marriage and career problems, and to keep the political outlook in line. The counselor served *in loco parentis*.

To Westerners, this all seems terribly intrusive. We feel that the individual needs to be left alone to work out such matters, or at least free to seek guidance if and when and from whomever he or she chooses. But much of this fine individualism evaporates in the workplace. There, we accept the wisdom that virtually everyone needs a firm direction, handed down from above. Most people do—they welcome a clear statement from the boss of just what specific targets are to be met in order to be considered a success. Most people need a well-defined charter, but managing the ones who don't is another matter.

The mark of the best manager is an ability to single out the few key spirits who have the proper mix of perspective and maturity and then turn them loose. Such a manager knows that he or she really can't give direction to these natural free electrons. They have progressed to the point where their own direction is more unerringly in the best interest of the organization than any direction that might come down from above. It's time to get out of their way.

39

Holgar Dansk

We have put this book together as a series of essays on the various ways that companies and projects go right and wrong. If we're on target, you should have been able to see your own situation reflected in at least a few of the essays. Each chapter, even the gloomiest, has had some prescriptive advice, something that you could do to begin the sensible reconstruction of a project, a division, or a whole organization. Of course, these prescriptions are inadequate, but they are a start. They encourage you to take on the Furniture Police, fight corporate entropy, defeat teamicidal tendencies, put more quality into the product (even if time *doesn't* permit), repeal Parkinson's Law, loosen up formal Methodologies, raise your E-Factor, open your kimono, and do a host of other things.

It doesn't take great prescience to see that one of these measures is all you're likely to pull off successfully. If you try more, you will just diffuse your efforts. The rumpus you'll raise will be more confusing than constructive, and your colleagues and those above you in the corporate hierarchy are likely to write you off as a whiner. One change is plenty. Even a single substantive change to the sociology of your organization will be a mammoth accomplishment.

But Why Me?

Making that single change is a tall order for one person. If you've got second thoughts about throwing yourself into the fray, it's only natural. Who are you, after all, to confront the kind of power group that springs up around the new Methodology or around the space and services being planned for the new office? Are you really strong enough?

Some years ago, there was a famous toreador who used the name El Cordobes. He was a charismatic fellow, and both his personal and professional lives were followed in the world press. In one interview, a reporter asked El Cordobes what regular exercises he did to stay fit enough for the ardors of bullfighting:

> "Exercises?"
> "Yes. You know, jogging or weight lifting, to maintain your physical condition."
> "There is something you don't understand, my friend. I don't wrestle the bull."

The key to success in fostering the kind of change we're advocating is that you not try to wrestle the bull. You're certainly not strong enough for that.

A single person acting alone is not likely to effect any meaningful change. But there's no need to act alone. When something is terribly out of kilter (like too much noise in the workplace), it takes very little to raise people's consciousness of it. Then it's no longer just you. It's everyone.

The Sleeping Giant

Just north of the Danish city of Copenhagen is the castle Kronborg. For the price of a few kroner, you can visit the castle casements and see there the reclining form of Holgar Dansk, the legendary sleeping giant of Denmark. He sleeps quietly while the country is at peace, but if ever Denmark should be in danger, Holgar will awake, and then his wrath will be terrible to see. Whole classes of Danish school children tiptoe down to see his 14-foot recumbent form. His shield and sword are there beside him, his armor ready to go. The children talk in whispers—nobody is too eager to see this giant in action, but they are happy he is on their side.

There may be a sleeping giant inside your own organization, ready to awaken when it is in danger. It is in danger if there is too much entropy, too little common sense. The giant is the body of your co-workers and subordinates, rational men and women whose patience is nearly exhausted. Whether they are great organizational thinkers or not, they know Silly when they see it. And some of the things that do most harm to the environment and sociology of the workplace are downright silly.

Waking Up Holgar

It doesn't take much to wake up the giant. If the silliness is gross enough, people need no more than a gentle catalyst. It may be one small voice saying, "This is unacceptable." People know it's true. Once it's been said out loud, they can't ignore it any longer.

That may seem idealistic, but if you do wake up a sleeping giant in your company, you won't be the first:

- An entire department of a large government agency has stuffed the bells in its old-fashioned telephones with tissues. There is no loud ringing now—only a gentle purr of clicks (or is it the quiet voice of Holgar Dansk?).

- A California computer company has had a rash of guerrilla attacks against the paging system in the programmer area. The wires keep getting cut. Because the programmers are seated in what used to be an assembly bay, the ceilings (and the paging-system speakers) are 16 feet up in the air. Who can even reach so high? Perhaps it was Holgar Dansk.

- The manager of a large project in Minneapolis has refused to move his people to the new quarters. ("New" in this case just meant smaller and noisier.) Administrators were simply stunned at his refusal; they had never considered the possibility. Working people are supposed to do as they're told. The manager had a different theory, that working people are supposed to do work. He had assembled enough evidence about the new environment to convince himself that they couldn't do that in the new workplace. So the proper function of the manager was to say no. If he had been all alone in taking this stand, it would have been easy to overrule him. But he wasn't alone. He had Holgar Dansk on his side.

- An Australian company doesn't form teams anymore but allows individuals to form their own. In that company, you join voluntarily with two of your colleagues and the company assigns the team as a unit. It might never have happened but for a little pressure from Holgar Dansk.

If you've smiled ruefully at any of the characterizations in this book, it's time now to stop smiling and start taking corrective action. Sociology matters more than technology or even money. It's supposed to be productive, satisfying fun to work. If it isn't, then there's nothing else worth concentrating on. Choose your terrain carefully, assemble your facts, and speak up. You can make a difference . . . with a little help from Holgar Dansk.

Index

Cottage-industry phenomenon, 231–232
Covert meaning of Methodology,
    176–177
Creative space, 75–76
Crosby, Philip, 22
Cult of quality, 168–169
Cultural diversity of food in team
    building, 110
Culture, corporate. *See* Corporate culture

D

Danish legislature, 86
Dansk, Holgar, 235–237
Data General project, 17
Day-care center, 220
de' Medici, Lorenzo, 204
Deadlines
    moving, 17
    as team obstacle, 148
    unreachable, 20
Death of a Salesman, 102
deBono, Edward, 144
Dedicated floor space and people density,
    53–54
Defect-prone design, 8
Defects
    defect density of software, 21
    noise factor in, 53
Defensiveness
    from error management, 8
    as team obstacle, 144–145
DeMarco, Tom, 183
Deming, W. Edwards, 157
Denver International Airport Baggage
    Handling System, 184–185
Deterministic systems, 175–176
Digital Equipment Corporation, PDP 11
    development at, 164
Direct physical oversight, 163
Dirksen, Everett, 121
Disposability feelings, turnover from, 120
Disruptions and disturbances
    flow factor, 62–64
    from fragmentation, 197
    getaways for, 164
    telephones, 67–71
Diversity in teams, 109–111
Do Not Disturb signs, 65

Documentary consistency, 225
Documentation in Methodologies, 178
Doors as success symbol, 73
Downsizing, 130
Dress codes, 95–96
DuPont, standardization at, 180
Dutch East India Company, 29

E

E-Factor, 64–65
E-mail
    corporate spam, 200
    FYIs, 200–201
    open organizations, 201
    passive consent, 201–202
    self-coordinating organizations, 202
    vs. telephone calls, 70
    time spent on, 199–200
    and young workers, 115
E-publications, borrowing, 184
Eagle project at Data General, 17
Early overstaffing, meetings from,
    194–196
Eating, communal, 88
Efficient production measures, 7
Efficient telephone schemes, 70–71
EG&G contractor, retraining at, 123
El Cordobes, 236
Eliteness in jelled teams, 136–137, 169–171
Emotions, 19
Employees
    as costs vs. capital, 125–130
    hiring. *See* Hiring
    parts view of, 9–10
    turnover. *See* Turnover
English Theory, 14
Enjoyment in jelled teams, 137
Entropy, corporate, 96–97
Environment. *See* Office environment
Environmental Factor, 64–65
Errors, dealing with, 8
Ethics in Philosophy, 218
Even Cowgirls Get the Blues (Robbins), 161
Expectations, articulating, 114–115
Expense vs. investment, 126
Experience
    as Coding War Games factor, 45
    learning from, 211–212